40 OBJECT LESSONS

40 OBJECT LESSONS

by Donald J. Poganski

Publishing House
St. Louis   London

Concordia Publishing House, St. Louis, Missouri
Concordia Publishing House Ltd., London E. C. 1
Copyright © 1973 Concordia Publishing House

Library of Congress Catalog Card No. 72-86233
International Standard Book No. 0-570-03148-6

MANUFACTURED IN THE UNITED STATES OF AMERICA

To
Doris

Index of Scripture Passages

10:2-4 — 82
13:55-56 — 145
15:19 — 48
16:24 — 80
17:5 — 93
24:9 — 51
24:10 — 51
25:14-46 — 107
25:16-23 — 100, 108
25:24-30 — 99, 108
25:30 — 37, 45, 147
25:31-46 — 68
25:34-40 — 97, 100
25:41-46 — 99
25:46 — 68, 100
26:26-28 — 81
27:3-5 — 98
28:19 — 119

Mark

3:16-19 — 82
6:4 — 145
6:17-24 — 98
10:13-16 — 97
12:41-44 — 72
14:22-24 — 81
16:15 — 63, 119

Luke

1:6 — 133
1:9-10 — 73
1:35 — 38, 45, 92
1:76-80 — 115
2:1-20 — 39

2:8-14 — 115
2:25 — 133
2:25-32 — 115
2:25-38 — 112
2:36-38 — 133
2:52 — 92
3:1-20 — 115
6:14-16 — 82
7:36-50 — 49
10:1-20 — 22, 120
10:20 — 59, 68
11:5-13 — 73
15 — 67
18:11-12 — 154
18:13 — 154
18:14 — 155
19:1-10 — 46, 78
21:25 — 52
21:26 — 52, 77
22:19-20 — 81
22:24-27 — 128
22:42 — 74
22:61-62 — 67
23:32-45 — 147
23:34 — 115
24:44-48 — 67
24:45-48 — 49
24:46-47 — 133

John

1:1 — 45
1:1-3 — 29
1:4-9 — 115
1:12 — 46
1:14 — 45
1:15 — 115

1:19-37 — 115
1:40-42 — 96
2:1-11 — 86
3:1-16 — 61
3:6 — 105, 127
3:13-15 — 21
3:14-17 — 152
3:16 — 63, 158
3:17-21 — 133
3:19 — 37
3:30 — 97
3:36 — 30, 67, 99, 148, 154, 158
4 — 117
4:23-24 — 30
4:46-54 — 152
5:24 — 61
5:24-25 — 148
5:29 — 68
6:5-7 — 83
6:8 — 96
6:27 — 26
8:12 — 115
8:31 — 32
8:31-32 — 56
8:36 — 32
9:14 — 107
10:14, 17 — 144
10:27-28 — 53
12:20-26 — 20
13 — 17 — 80
13:34-35 — 93, 144
14:6 — 158
14:16-17 — 61
15:3 — 81
15:18-19 — 53

9

10

11

Contents

14

Preface

Teaching goes better with visuals. The hearer's attention is attracted and held so that the seed of the Word can be planted in the heart. Then, as our Savior promised, "They are those who, hearing the Word, hold it fast in an honest and good heart and bring forth fruit with patience." (Luke 8:15)

This volume of visual sermonettes includes a wide variety of object visuals applied to numerous Bible texts and accounts. Some of the lessons have been given as children's talks in the Sunday services. Some were visual sermons that have been condensed. Some were given as devotions at Sunday school and vacation Bible school openings and also at youth gatherings.

The lessons are easily adapted to any age level. Pastors, teachers, topic and devotional leaders will find them helpful. The objects are easy to get and prepare.

Texts are listed with lesson titles in the table of contents. A more detailed listing of all Bible passages is given in the index. Any number of texts may be used as support material for the lesson or additional ideas for a particular visual.

A special note is in order for pastors. Some of the lessons may be enlarged for sermons in the congregational worship setting. Suggested ones are numbers 2, 3, 4, 5, 10, 14, 16, 18, 19, 25, and 31. Also others may be used as sermon approaches.

All Scripture quotations are from the Revised Standard Version unless otherwise indicated.

It is my prayer that you will enjoy sharing the Good News by means of visuals and that many people will be reached and edified and be led to "grow in the grace and knowledge of our Lord and Savior Jesus Christ." (2 Peter 3:18)

D. J. P.

A LOOK THAT SAVES

Materials: Make a heart by folding an 8½" by 11" white piece of paper from each end to center, leaving about ½" open in the center. Be sure to leave plenty of paper for hinges. Paste red paper on the front flaps. Write the name *JESUS* downward in the ½" center portion. At the *E* write *EY* on the left side and *S* on the right side. This will make the words *YES* and *EYES*. Make one fold in the left flap at the hinge, large enough to expose the *Y* so that the word *YES* can be seen as you hinge back the right flap.

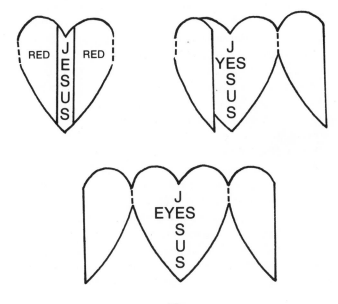

The Bible tells us that when Jesus forgives us He also gives us a new heart. (Display the white heart from back side.) The Bible tells us that Jesus then dwells in our hearts in a spiritual or mystical way\(Eph. 3:16-17; Rev. 3:20). (Show the front of the heart with the name JESUS on it.) This reminds us that Jesus is at the controls of the desires of our hearts, as He is in the center of our hearts.

What does the name Jesus mean? The angel told Joseph what name God Himself chose for His Son who would be born of the Virgin Mary. "You shall call His name Jesus, for He will save His people from their sins" (Matt. 1:21). So "Jesus" means "Savior." Jesus is the God-man who was able to shed His blood. By that blood He is able to save the whole world from the eternal death penalty of sin. The red which covers this heart assures us of that truth. (1 John 1:7)

(Expose the YES.) Here is another word. It is the word YES. This word means assent, agreement, and acceptance. Being Christians means that we are continually saying yes to Jesus in a living act of faith. (Open the left flap all the way to make the word EYES.) Saying yes to Jesus is really seeing Him with "eyes" of faith. We see physical objects with our physical eyes. But there is a sense in which we see with "inner eyes" of the heart. That is the spiritual seeing of faith worked by the Holy Spirit.

What do you see about Jesus? To see His beauty as the sinless Son of God is indeed wonderful. That inspires our imagination toward holiness. To see His kindness and concern is also precious. That inspires us toward kindness. But there is something more central and basic that we must continually see about Jesus. It is very evident right before your eyes. See how a cross is formed by the crossing of the words EYES and JESUS. So seeing Jesus with eyes of faith means to trust His life-giving Calvary love that takes away our death penalty. (John 12:20-26)

My faith looks up to Thee,
Thou Lamb of Calvary,
Savior Divine.
Now hear me while I pray;
Take all my guilt away;
Oh, let me from this day
Be wholly Thine!
(*The Lutheran Hymnal,* 394)

Once when the people of Israel became discouraged in their journey, they grumbled against God, saying, "We loathe this worthless food [manna]" (Num. 21:5). God sent fiery serpents among the people to bring them to repentance. The serpents had a deadly bite. Many of the people that were bitten died. But others began to feel sorry for their sins of grumbling and ingratitude against God. They asked Moses to pray God for their deliverance. God heard Moses' prayer. God instructed Moses to erect a pole and attach a bronze serpent on it as a symbol. Then if any bitten person would look on that serpent he would live. This looking was an act of taking God at His word, which is what faith is. God did the healing. This serpent on the pole was a type of Jesus Christ (John 3:13-15). Looking to Jesus means the looking of faith which accepts forgiveness.

There are some clear lessons for life in this looking to Jesus. We are not to look at our "pet" sins and consider them mere harmless pastimes. This only leads to ruin. Rather faith in Jesus, who is our Pioneer and Perfecter, leads to daily victory (Heb. 12:1-3). We are not to dwell on our hurts and troubles in life. This only causes a neurotic obsession with them. If the people of Israel had kept looking on their bites they would have died. We are healed and whole as we look to Jesus. We are not to look upon either our failures or successes in Kingdom work. Failure would lead to despair, and success to pride. Jesus directed some success-happy disciples away from it to their ultimate glory in Him (Luke 10:1-20). We are to look only to Jesus. He keeps our faith strong.

ADDING COLOR
TO YOUR PRAYER LIFE

Materials: Nine candles placed in a holder to make candles ascend from the center. Candles are to be of the following colors to represent the introduction, seven petitions, and conclusion of the Lord's Prayer: blue, white, violet, green, yellow, red, gray, gold, and orange (other colors may be substituted). Begin presentation with blue candle burning. Place each candle in holder and light as needed during the presentation.

Does the Lord's Prayer become just words that we say in a hurry? We hardly think about what we are praying and so we abuse this prayer. Luther said that the Lord's Prayer is the greatest martyr. That we can better think of what we are praying, why not think of the various parts of the Lord's Prayer by a different colored candle? (Matt. 6:9-13)

"Our Father who art in heaven" is the beginning, or introduction, to the Lord's Prayer. The burning candle reminds us that God is light, in whom is no darkness at all. James said it like this: "Every good endowment and every perfect gift is from above, coming down from the Father of lights, with whom there is no variation or shadow due to change" (James 1:17). The blue candle reminds us that our Father is our heavenly Father. Blue stands for the blue above where Jesus ascended. We pray confidently as sons, knowing that our Father will not spoil us with trinkets of time but answer our prayers in line with the treasures of eternity.

(Light the white candle.) White is the color of holiness and purity. We pray, "Hallowed be Thy name." "Hallowed" is an old word that means holy. We are asking that God's name be holy with us. God's name stands for more than just the word "God." It stands for every revelation of God in the Bible and every holy ordinance. Using the name of God in a holy way calls us to give up phoniness and to be Christians for real. It also calls us to urgency, conviction, and newness of living, as Jesus said, "Let your light so shine before men." (Matt. 5:16)

(Light the violet candle.) Violet stands for repentance. True sorrow for our sins and trust in Jesus for forgiveness is the only way to enter God's kingdom and remain members of it. We want Christ to rule our hearts in this time of grace so we may finally be with Him in His kingdom of glory. In this prayer we promise to share His Word with others for the building of His kingdom. It is our mission prayer.

(Light the green candle.) Green is the color of eternal life, as we are reminded by evergreen trees. If there is one word that summarizes our Father's will for us, it is the word "life"; "This is the will of My Father, that every one who sees the Son and believes in Him should have eternal life" (John 6:40). So we pray, "Thy will be done on earth as it is in heaven." Enemies of our faith want to rob us of God's will. But we want to imitate angels in doing God's will. We are really promising to give earnest heed to feeding our souls on His living Word to remain strong and possess eternal life.

(Light the yellow candle.) This candle reminds us of earth and golden fields of ripened grain. It stands for our daily bread. Our Father gives daily bread through honest labor, for He is the Giver of every endowment. We receive our daily bread in faith and with thanksgiving. We are thankful for the basic things of life and do not grumble when we don't have the candies, cokes, and ice-cream cones of life. We need not worry about tomorrow, for we know we can depend on our Father for daily bread. So we pray, "Give us this day our daily bread."

(Light the red candle.) Red stands for the blood of Christ, the complete payment for the eternal debt of sin. There is forgiveness through Christ. Our greatest need is having forgiveness, so we pray, "And forgive us our debts." When we experience the joy of His forgiveness, knowing He forgives the eternal debt of sin we could never pay, we promise to forgive others their little debts to us. In fact we have already forgiven them in the act of believing in Christ's forgiveness, and so we pray, "As we also have forgiven our debtors."

(Light the gray candle.) Gray stands for temptations by the devil, the world, and our flesh. Trials and troubles are tests by which our Father strengthens our faith and improves our love. Our enemies would want us to doubt and lose faith. The greatest evil is to die in one's sins. Gray stands for unbelief. We want to be saved from that tragedy. We need our Father's help, so we pray, "And lead us not into temptation," which means, "Save us from unbelief in the time of trial," or, "Keep our faith glowing amid' temptations."

(Light the gold candle.) Gold stands for heaven described as a precious, golden city of eternal security and glory. We want to be faithful at all times. Our Father will finally take us from earth with its trials to heaven with its glory. So we pray, "But deliver us from evil." In heaven we will not be concerned with falling into the evil of unbelief. We will walk in the light of God by sight.

(Light the orange candle.) This is the color of a golden sunset, the reflection of glory. If the light of the sunset is so beautiful, what must the true light of our Father in heaven be like! So we add a conclusion, "For thine is the kingdom and the power and the glory forever. Amen." (RSV footnote. The conclusion is not found in most of the ancient manuscripts. It comes from 1 Chron. 29:11.)

Let us look at the arrangement of these candles that make up the Lord's Prayer. Notice how the middle candle is lowest. It touches our earthly needs. Besides it is protected on each side by four candles of spiritual needs. We are not to become sod-bound, earthly, and obsessed with the things of time. If we really pray the thoughts and truths of this prayer, we will not fall in love with this world. Jesus said something about this in John 6:27 and Matt. 4:4. Jesus put a "heavenly hedge" around our prayer for bodily things so we wouldn't get carried away by their attraction. It puts earthly things in their rightful place, as Jesus taught in Matt. 6:33: "Seek first His kingdom and His righteousness, and all these things shall be yours as well."

When you pray the Lord's Prayer, let these burning candles of various color appear in your mind's eye and then really think about what you pray.

Think of one of the prayers in the Bible (Dan. 9:17-19). Compare it to the Lord's Prayer. What "colors" stand out?

ALL ABOUT CHRISTIANITY

Materials: 1. One large ship made according to directions in illustration. The paper must be twice as long as wide. The ship is made with the same folds as making a paper hat, except that more paper is folded into it to make the top of the cross when the ship is cut. Label the ship **WORLD.** On the reverse side draw a tombstone.

2. A number of small ships cut out of posterboard on which are written *WORSHIP, MEMBERSHIP, STEWARD-SHIP, FELLOWSHIP, PARTNERSHIP* in black letters. Black letters depict them as works of the Law. On the reverse side write the same words in red to depict works of faith and love.

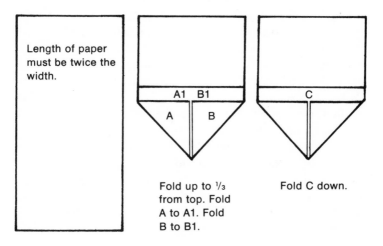

Length of paper must be twice the width.

Fold up to ⅓ from top. Fold A to A1. Fold B to B1.

Fold C down.

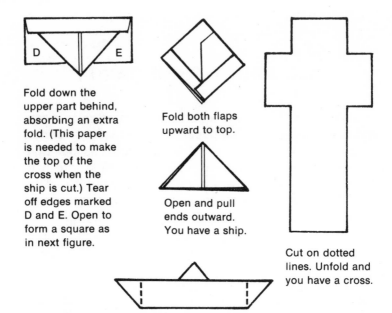

Fold down the upper part behind, absorbing an extra fold. (This paper is needed to make the top of the cross when the ship is cut.) Tear off edges marked D and E. Open to form a square as in next figure.

Fold both flaps upward to top.

Open and pull ends outward. You have a ship.

Cut on dotted lines. Unfold and you have a cross.

(Hold up the ship.) Our world is like a ship. It is sailing along in space. Destination is unknown to the world by itself. The ship of the world is grand and beautiful in its makeup. People on the ship are gifted with scientific genius. People know a lot about the makeup and workings of the ship. (Name some of the latest scientific ventures.) Yet the world is without chart and compass. It just drifts along without destination. Life for the people on the ship is short —"threescore years and ten." It is observed that the young may die and the old must die. People on the ship live out their lives in the midst of trouble. Change and decay is all around. It is like a sailing cemetery, with tombstones and men's bones. (Show reverse side.) People engage in strife, hatred, and immorality in an effort to satisfy their sinful desires. Yet there is something in the hearts of all people which tells them that someday, all too soon, the trip will be over. And then eternity! But where? God has put eternity in men's minds in the sense that people have consciences which tell them that not all is right between them and God (Rom. 2:14-16). Without faith in Christ people can only live in the fear of the unknown, the fear of living, and the fear of dying. (Heb. 2:15)

Motivated by fear, some people devise little ships. They want to bail out, as it were, onto the sea of life in the hope of finding a destination or being rescued. (Pull out ships one by one; display during remarks; then drop as if to make it sink.) Some try WORSHIP. Man is a worshiping creature by nature. He worships some kind of a god, even if it be the god of self (Rom. 1:20-25). The ship sinks. Some try MEMBERSHIP, getting outwardly connected with a group called the church. It sinks. Some try STEWARDSHIP, but practice only token giving—a dollar now and then for charity, just in case. It sinks. Some try FELLOWSHIP, being involved in a church function, benefit, or social effort. It sinks. Others try PARTNERSHIP, going along with God in a religious way to a point, like a business partner, but making sure that God does not impose His will on theirs. All such human efforts to make things right between them and God are vain. They are not seaworthy. (Gal. 3:10-11a)

Yet all along, the way to get right with God and the chart and compass to the safe destination of eternal life are revealed to the world. That revelation God has given to the world by His Word (Heb. 1:1-4; John 1:1-3). (Cut off the ends of the ship and unfold.) What? A cross? What does it mean? Listen. "Christ redeemed us from the curse of the Law, having become a curse for us" (Gal. 3:13). And, "He who through faith is righteous shall live." (Gal. 3:11)

People who take the message of the cross seriously and believe find forgiveness, peace, and security in Christ.

They live above fear in the certain hope of everlasting life. They live out their lives of faith in great thanksgiving. They do good works to thank God for His love. They use the little ships, but for a redeeming purpose (Eph. 5:15-16). They want to thank God by sharing the good news about the cross of Christ. (Attach ships, the side with words in red, with paper clips to the arms of the cross.) WORSHIP is from the heart as a living response of faith (John 4:23-24). MEMBERSHIP is belonging to the body of Christ, the church, by the power of the Holy Spirit (1 Cor. 12:12-13). STEWARDSHIP is the giving of entire self to the new management of the Holy Spirit to the glory of God (1 Cor. 6:19-20). FELLOWSHIP is in the functioning bond of oneness in Christ (Acts 2:42). PARTNERSHIP is putting God first in everything. It is living in the attitude of prayer — "Father, Thy will be done." Our good works of course are not perfect, but God accepts them because they are done in faith. He mightily blesses them so that the message of salvation in Christ, His Son, might be shared with others. The goal of life is found only in Christ (John 3:36). Christians are busy calling out that message to the lost. The answer to life is in the cross of Calvary (Heb. 1:1-4; 2:14-18). God has revealed the only rescue procedure to the world. This is what Christianity is all about.

BANNERS OF VICTORY

Materials: An American flag and a Christian flag. Small-size flags that can be held in the hand are best.

(Display the American flag.) Do you know when the "Stars and Stripes" became the flag of our country? Our land became a nation on July 4, 1776. It was less than a year afterwards that the Continental Congress adopted this design of the American flag—June 14, 1777. This day is known as Flag Day each year. A country needs a flag, or banner, as a symbol of its convictions.

George Washington said that we take the star from heaven, the red from the mother country, separating it by white stripes, thus showing that we have separated from it, and the white stripes shall go down to posterity representing liberty. The colors have a very practical meaning. The red stands for courage and sacrifice. White stands for purity. It expresses the basic fact that "righteousness exalts a nation, but sin is a reproach to any people" (Prov. 14:34). Blue, the color of the heavens, stands for loyalty. It reminds us that we owe loyalty to God and His truth. The stars representing the states are set in a field of blue. This expresses the thought that as God holds the stars in the heavens, so He alone must hold the states together in one strong nation.

The Stars and Stripes stands for our precious civil liberty. But civil liberty has its source in a greater liberty, that is, spiritual. Jesus said: "If you continue in My Word, you are truly My disciples, and you will know the truth,

31

and the truth will make you free" (John 8:31). (Display the Christian flag.) The colors correspond to the colors of the American flag. Civil liberty has its source in spiritual liberty. The red cross reminds us that Jesus Christ, God's Son, freed every person from the eternal death penalty of sin. On the cross He suffered and died and experienced what every sinner deserves. He took the penalty on Himself. That's why He could say: "If the Son makes you free, you will be free indeed" (John 8:36). The cross is on a field of blue. It is the color of the unclouded sky or heavens above. It stands for sincerity and loyal faith in Christ. We not only call Him Savior. We also call Him Lord and Master. We understand that "He died for all, that those who live might live no longer for themselves but for Him who for their sake died and was raised" (2 Cor. 5:15). The large field is white. It reminds us that by believing in Jesus Christ we are pure in God's sight, covered with Christ's blood-bought holiness. This fits us for heaven. We then let Christ make a real difference in our living in our practice of purity. White also stands for peace. White is recognized as a flag of truce on battlefields. There is enmity and strife between man and God because of sin, but the white of Christ's holiness, which is the believer's by faith, brings the assurance of peace. The believers are therefore the peacemakers and live as the pure in heart. (Matt. 5:8-9)

There is a story that the Christian flag was envisioned by a Sunday school superintendent, Mr. Charles C. Overton of Brighton Chapel, Coney Island, Sept. 26, 1897. He was inspired by the American flag and drew up a design of the Christian flag to show the source of liberty and to stand as a reminder of every Christian's allegiance to Christ.*

* Nevada M. Whitwell, *At Home and Abroad* (The Standard Publishing Co., Cincinnati, Ohio, 1952) p. 95.

32

The idea of using a flag to symbolize allegiance to truth in a march for victory is not an American idea or Mr. Overton's idea. It goes back to God Himself: "Thou hast set up a banner for those who fear Thee, to rally to it from the bow [truth]" (Ps. 60:4). And, "May we shout for joy over your victory, and in the name of our God set up our banners" (Ps. 20:5). The banner refers to a flag. God has committed such a standard to His people that they might go forth as soldiers of His cause. His people fight against godless enemies so that a righteous cause may be promoted and the honor of the true God upheld. We as Christians are loyal to Christ out of love. As we serve Him, our loyalty brings benefit to our nation. We live in daily victory over evils that seek to destroy us.

If we want a strong nation loyal to God and His truth, we must always go to the source of that power, the spiritual liberty in Christ. "If we are not controlled by God, then we will be governed by tyrants," was the way William Penn put it. Our banners stand for the fact that we realize our need for God's control both in the spiritual and civil realm.

I think of the idea of setting up banners of victory in the name of our God when I read about loyal Moses (Heb. 11:23-28; see the story of his victorious life recorded in Exodus). I think of the victorious Joseph who put up banners of his God in red, white, and blue (Gen. 39:6-23). I think of Daniel and his three friends at Babylon who set up their banners in the name of God. They refused to compromise even in matters of diet, not to speak of prayer and worship of the true God. (Daniel 1; 3; 6)

One more thing: the flagpole points to heaven. This is the goal of life. God wants us to live in the light, life, and liberty of heaven already now as we fight the good fight of faith. (Rom. 8:31-39; 2 Tim. 4:6-8)

BASIC CHRISTIAN TRUTH

Materials: A cassock, surplice, stole, clerical collar, and cross. If you are a pastor, put them on piece by piece during the demonstration. You may wear the collar from the beginning if you prefer. If you are a teacher, perhaps you can borrow them from the pastor for display during your presentation. (Psalm 51 is used as a basis.)

(Put on the cassock.) Do you know the name for this part of the clerical vestments? It is called a cassock. Notice that it covers my body from "head to toe." Open your Bibles to Psalm 51. Notice the words King David uses for that which is basically wrong with his heart: "transgressions, iniquity, sin, evil." He adds that it is something that came to him as a hand-me-down of nature (v. 5). This caused him to do such horrible sins as murder and adultery (2 Samuel 11 and 12). The color of the cassock proclaims that everyone is sinful by nature from "head to toe." The cassock reminds us that we must own up to our sinfulness as sin against God (v. 4). Compare Rom. 3:9-20. Our worship includes owning up to sinfulness. Christianity is the religion of the broken heart, broken with sorrow over sinning against God. (V. 17)

(Put on surplice.) Who knows the name of this part of the vestments? It is called a surplice. It is white to remind us that there is forgiveness through the mercy of God. (The mercy comes to all people through the suffering and death of Jesus on the cross — clerical cross over the surplice shows how God is forgiving to sinners.) As the surplice covers the cassock, so the righteousness of Christ covers our guilt of sin before God. The king prayed: "Have mercy on me, O God, according to Thy steadfast love" (v. 1). He prayed: "Wash me . . . cleanse me . . . purge me . . . and I shall be whiter than snow" (vv. 2, 7). In King David's time the coming of Christ was evidenced in ceremonies where sacrificial animal blood was mixed with hyssop for purification. People believed in the coming Savior. In the New Testament there is in the blood shed by the Lamb of God once for all forgiveness to all who believe. The white surplice invites us to come to God for cleansing. God for Christ's sake pronounces sinners who believe forgiven. This puts joy and gladness in our hearts (v. 8). The surplice reminds us of these happy things that come from being forgiven people. It also reminds us to strive to live as new people (vv. 10-12). The power comes from faith which trusts His forgiveness. We aim to live out what we are in His sight by faith. Sin has to give up its control. The king asked God's help so he would not do the sins over again. (V. 14)

(Put on stole.) This is called a stole. It fits like a yoke around my neck. Oxen pull a burden by means of a yoke. The pastor's "burden" is to proclaim the basic truths of salvation, Law and Gospel, sin and grace. The pastor is the public teacher of the church. Everyone who is a Christian takes the lead from the pastor and teaches privately. When anyone experiences the basic truths for newness of life, there is inner desire to share them. "Then I will teach transgressors Thy ways, and sinners will return to Thee" (v. 13). This has been called the prayer of the Sunday school teacher. Christian teachers must have a sin-and-grace experience to be good teachers. The stole changes colors with the various seasons of the church year. (Comment on the symbolic meaning of the colors.) The stole reminds us that the whole message of Christ is to be proclaimed as expressed in His birth, life, suffering, death, resurrection, ascension, and second coming in connection with the whole truth of the Triune God. The stole is the invitation for everyone to be yoked more completely to Christ by being daily students of His Word. (2 Peter 3:18)

(Refer to the clerical collar.) This collar is round and in a way resembles a handcuff. In days of old slaves were "neck-cuffed" by a collar to which a chain was attached. The apostle Paul called himself a prisoner of Jesus (Eph. 3:1). The clerical collar is a picture of the captive heart for Christ. Like pastor, like people. We are about the Lord's business as a way of life. King David got busy living life as a thankoffering of love. He shouted praise and asked for power to live with his heart captive to God (vv. 15-16). He got busy with Kingdom work, which he had neglected to do, and took interest in building the walls around the holy city (v. 18). He would continue to take an active part in public worship too (v. 19). The clerical collar is white to remind us that service done by captive hearts is done in the power of faith. We are God's cleansed people, and we aim to praise Him with holiness of living as servants of Christ.

Clerical vestments are a visual sermon proclaiming the basic truths of our Christian faith. Clerical vestments were God's idea (Exodus 28). They cover the preacher as a person in order to give added impetus to the proclamation. Designs differ in various denominations. The vestments around which this lesson is built are used in many churches.

BETHLEHEM OF MY HEART

Materials: A large manila envelope. On one side place a symbol of a manger near the bottom and a red cross near the top. (If available, a manger-scene picture may be used in place of the manger symbol.) Put a divider inside the envelope to make it a double. Paste the top and bottom edges of the divider to the envelope. Before pasting, place a white heart inside the section with symbols. The heart should be as large as the envelope. You will need a gray heart the same size which will be later placed into the other side of the envelope and sealed. Have a letter opener handy to open the side with the white heart.

God is light, and in Him is no darkness at all. We might think of His light as white, for God is holy. In contrast to that holiness, man is sinful. (Display gray heart.) The apostle John wrote: "This is the judgment, that the light has come into the world, and men loved darkness rather than light, because their deeds were evil" (John 3:19). If nothing happens to change this, then there is the ultimate darkness of eternal death, as Jesus said: "Cast the worthless servant into the outer darkness" (Matt. 25:30). So this large, gray heart represents human sinfulness (Eccl. 7:20) with its ultimate eternal death.

Is it possible that a change can occur? That is what Christmas is all about. (Display the envelope.) Look at the manger event. In the little town of Bethlehem it happened. What the prophet Micah predicted in such minute detail centuries before came to pass: "But you, O Bethlehem

37

Ephrathah [fruitful one], who are little to be among the clans of Judah, from you shall come forth for Me One who is to be ruler in Israel, whose origin is from of old, from ancient days" (Micah 5:2). (Compare Is. 7:14; 9:6-7.)

> True Son of the Father,
> He comes from the skies;
> To be born of a virgin
> He doth not despise.
> (*The Lutheran Hymnal,* 102)

Pause to ponder the miracle of the manger. A town so tiny; a miracle so great! So lowly a mother; so glorious a Son (Luke 1:35)! So ordinary an event; so wondrous a result! The result is salvation for the whole world through the birth of this one Baby. The angel said in announcing the Savior's birth: "He will save His people from their sins" (Matt. 1:21). Thus behind the manger is the cross. He came as true man so He could shed His precious blood in redemption. He picked up the death penalty of the world and carried it in His holy body and soul to the cross. In those God-forsaken moments of darkness He was made a curse in the sinners' place.

All this would remain mere history unless something happens in the hearts of sinful people. When we are sick of sin, when we feel the poverty of our spirits, when we know our spiritual need for God's love and light in the face of God's law, then we respond to God's invitation of love: Come! Come just as you are. Do you want His love and light? This gray heart represents your heart and the heart of anyone who comes. (Insert it in the envelope, God's salvation plan, and seal it.) The penalty of sin is transferred to Jesus. You and I are not to concern ourselves with it at all. When God forgives, He remembers our sins no more (Ps. 103:12). When God forgives, He also gives. (Open the envelope for the white heart.) This is what God gives, a new heart! Thus Jesus must be born in our hearts by faith for a life of peace, joy, and light. Someone has said:

"Though Christ be in Bethlehem a thousand times born,
Until He is born in you, you are yet forlorn."

It must be a Bethlehem of my heart.

Bethlehem means "House of Bread." It was a fruitful valley where wheatfields waved in the sun. Truly, from that valley and lowly town came the Bread of Life for hungry souls. No one can live without Him. Let us renew our faith today as we prayerfully ponder the personal meaning of the manger:

How silently, how silently,
The wondrous Gift is giv'n!
So God imparts to human hearts
The blessings of His heav'n
No ear may hear His coming,
But in this world of sin,
Where meek souls will receive Him still,
The dear Christ enters in.

O holy Child of Bethlehem,
Descend to us, we pray;
Cast out our sin and enter in,
Be born in us today.
We hear the Christmas angels
The great glad tidings tell:
Oh, come to us, abide with us,
Our Lord Immanuel!
(*The Lutheran Hymnal,* 647)

We can learn more about the coming of God's Son by reading the Christmas accounts. (Luke 2:1-20; Matt. 1:18-25; Titus 2:11-14; Gal. 4:4-7)

39

CHRIST IS THE ANSWER

Materials: Four boxes. Two of them should be white and the same size (the top and bottom of the same box). Suggested size: 6″ by 6″ by 3″. Label the side of the top section *GOD* in green letters. Label the side of the bottom section *CHRIST* in green. Place a red cross on the bottom of the *CHRIST* box the full size of the box. The third box should be smaller. Label the bottom "me" in black letters. On the sides write "sin" and "death." The fourth box is the one to be used to express the false teaching at Colossae. This box should be midway in size between the *GOD* box and the "me" box. It should be off-white. Label it "christ." Have the *CHRIST* box inside the *GOD* box before you begin the lesson. Also write the word *FATHER* on the side of the *GOD* box, as the open part is upward.

(Display GOD box.) This box is white and is labeled GOD. What does white tell us about God? Indeed, that holiness and purity belong to God in an absolute way. The letters are in green. What does that suggest about God? It suggests that God is eternal. Green, like an evergreen tree, that God is everlasting.

(Display "me" box.) What difference do you see between these two boxes? Color is different. Letters are different in size and color. These differences remind us that something is basically wrong in the hearts of people by nature. What is it? It's written on the sides. Sin, and the wages of sin, which is death. Thus we can see that GOD and little "me" are opposites. The sad fact is that you and I can do nothing to change the situation. It's all up to God.

God did act to change the sad situation. He gave His Son, who was one with the Father from eternity. (Bring out CHRIST box and place it below the GOD box.) Notice that both are the same in size and colors. Christ is holy and eternal, like the Father and the Holy Spirit. Christ is the official title for God's Son in His saving mission. It means He was set aside as the Prophet, Priest, and King of salvation. Christ is God. The apostle Paul stressed this when he wrote to Christians at Colossae: "He is the image of the invisible God . . . in Him all the fullness of God was pleased to dwell, and through Him to reconcile to Himself all things, whether on earth or in heaven, making peace by the blood of His cross" (Col. 1:15-20). Because Christ is God, He can save sinful people by shedding His blood on the cross. In fact He can save the whole world. He is the divine "Go-between" between the holy God and sinful people. Notice the red cross on the CHRIST box. It reminds us of His saving work. Whoever believes in Christ is reconciled personally with God. The apostle speaks of this in Col. 1:21-23.

(Place the "me" box in the CHRIST box.) When we believe in Christ, we are in Christ and covered with His holiness. God sees us as holy as His dear Son. And there is more! We are made friends of God for a living companionship. (Place the CHRIST box inside the GOD box and show the name FATHER.) We are secure in Christ. God is our Father. The apostle wrote: "You have died, and your life is hid with Christ in God" (Col. 3:3). There's more to come on Judgment Day. We will appear with Christ in glory perfected in His holiness. (Col. 3:4)

This is the message Paul preached at Colossae. In it

41

the believers found their joyous salvation in Christ. But false teachers came into their midst. They were known as "Gnostics" a name that came from the Greek word "to know." They acted like spiritual "wise-guys" who had all the answers. They probed into the question of how evil might have come into the world. They wanted to figure it out logically. They accepted the fact that God is holy. (Show GOD box.) But they could not understand how a holy God could end up with an imperfect, unholy universe. They looked around at the "immoral mess" and said, "This is beneath God's dignity," or something like that. So they figured it out like this: God, the supreme Maker, created a number of spirits which He charged with rulership. These in turn became less perfect down the line, and then some of the least perfect spirits came up with an imperfect universe. They were even willing to think of Christ as one of these lesser spirits, although somewhat holier. In Colossians these spirits are called, "elemental spirits of the universe" (2:8). (Place the off-white "christ" box below the GOD box.) See the difference they came up with. To them Christ was much less than God. Being imperfect and less than God, how could He save anyone? Well, these "know-it-alls" had to go a step farther. Since they denied the saving power of Christ's cross, they insisted on a "do-it-yourself-styled" religion. A sample of this is in Col. 2:16-23.

(Throw the off-white "christ" box aside.) Read Col. 2:9: "For in Him the whole fullness of deity dwells bodily, and you have come to fullness of life in Him, who is the head of all rule and authority." (Display the CHRIST box and put it in the GOD box as before.)

Christ is true God; therefore He is the answer to everything. He guides us according to His eternal plan. That plan is solidly anchored in what Christ is (2:9), what Christ has done (1:20; 2:13-14), and the position Christ occupies (3:1). What our lives should be like in view of this plan is the content of the apostle's prayer in 1:9-14.

CHRIST SHARED OUR SINS

Materials: A large letter "I" (12″ high) made of corrugated cardboard. The "I" should be in gray. The letters "S" and "N" 3″ high in brown. Attach to paddle-bar stick and insert into the letter "I" to spell "SIN." A large letter "I" in white (12″ high) on which is pasted a green letter "O" the same size as the "S" and "N." When this letter is placed over the gray "I," the word "SON" appears. A child of about 7–12 years of age should be employed in the lesson.

(Ask the child to answer the following questions:)

Suppose you were at a check-out counter at a store. The person ahead of you lost some money. You saw it fall to the floor. What would be your first thought? (Quite naturally it would be to keep it.)

Suppose you didn't know an answer on a test. The answer could be easily gotten from a classmate. What would be your first reaction? (To cheat would be a natural reaction.)

Suppose someone is angry with you and calls you a terrible name. What would be your first thought? (Wouldn't it be to call a worse name back?)

Suppose there's but one piece of cake left. You are very hungry. There are others in your home. What is your first inclination? (Forget about others!)

What does the Bible call stealing, cheating, name-calling, selfishness? (Display the sIN object.) Someone suggested that we must spell sin like this with a big *I* so that each one of us will have to admit, "Yes, I sin." The apostle Paul "spelled" it that way, calling himself chief of sinners, or foremost of sinners (1 Tim. 1:15). The final outcome of sin is eternal death. Gray stands for the eternal darkness where God is not (Matt. 25:30). The capital *I* stands for our person, or "ego," that our entire nature is sold under sin – its penalty, power, and punishment.

God acted in love to rescue us from the bondage of sin. He sent His Son. (Show the white letter *I* with green *O*.) The large *I* stands for God's Son. It is in white because God's Son is holy (Luke 1:35). The green *O* reminds us that He is eternal. "In the beginning was the Word . . . and the Word was God" (John 1:1). The Son of God stepped down to earth to save. The Son of God became the Son of Man. (Place the white *I* over the gray *I*.) Now you can read the word SON. He took upon Himself real flesh, the dust of the earth, flesh (represented by the brown), yet without its decay. So the Eternal One became flesh in time. "The Word became flesh and dwelt among us, full of grace and truth" (John 1:14). He came to bring the grace of deliverance to sin-bound people.

This action is explained for us in Phil. 2:5-11: "Being found in human form He humbled Himself and became obedient unto death, even death on a cross." (Bend the top part of the *I* letters forward and the shape of the cross appears.) On that cross Jesus Christ became sin for us. He was treated as all lost sinners should be treated. He became completely involved in the death penalty of every person. He was forsaken by His Father to taste eternal death for every person. He as the sinless One could effectively save sinners because His divine nature was involved in His atoning work. That's why He could redeem the whole world (2 Cor. 5:17-21). By faith in God's Son we become what He is – holy sons of God. Gal. 4:4-7 assures us that God's Son

45

acted so that we might receive the adoption of sons. (See John 1:12.) He became what we are that we might become what He is. The green *O* reminds us of our gift of eternal life that we have in Christ.

As sons we strive to live in a way that agrees with our sonship. Because we belong to Christ, we crucify our old nature of sin. We let Christ control our daily living. (1 John 2:2-6)

This was the understanding the apostles John and Paul had about their sonship. When we have experienced the changeover from SIN-slaves to sons of God in Christ, we aim to live as the sons of God.

Zacchaeus (Luke 19:1-10), Matthew (Matt. 9:9), and a whole group of Old Testament people (Heb. 11) can testify to this changeover. Do you?

CLEANSED FROM SIN

Materials: Three liquids: (1) A "scarlet" liquid made from two solutions: One tbsp. of washing soda added to a cup of water; and one Bromo Quinine cold tablet in a cup of water brought to boiling point. (Decant the clear liquid to be used in the demonstration.) Mix the two solutions together. Place in a pint jar with large mouth. Paste an outline of a heart in green on the front side of jar. Paste white paper on back side of jar. (This will add more whiteness to the clear liquid when it is turned to clear.) (2) Half cup water. This is added to the "scarlet" solution during the demonstration to represent the futility of the human effort to effect a change. (Allow enough room in the pint jar for the amount of water you wish to use, and also for the next liquid.) (3) One-fourth cup white distilled vinegar. Attach a wooden cross (size to fit into the pint jar) to a container large enough to hold the vinegar. Place container at base of cross. The vinegar will turn the "scarlet" liquid clear.

This jar will represent the hearts and souls of all human beings. The green outline reminds us that our souls are immortal and undying and will exist always. This is terribly frightening because our souls lack spiritual life, are under condemnation, and would exist apart from God eternally unless something happened to change that. God has given His diagnosis of the human soul in Is. 1:18: "Your sins are like scarlet . . . like crimson." Just what is God saying by such descriptions? Makers of scarlet cloth in olden days dyed the cloth in the grain and then in the piece. It was twice-dyed! We are sinners "twice-dyed," sinners by nature and sinners by practice. King David admitted this in Ps. 51:5. The apostle Paul wrote about it in Rom. 5:12: "Death spread to all men because all men sinned." Sins of practice come from the condition of the heart, as Jesus said in Matt. 15:19. Also, the description of scarlet tells us how completely helpless we are to do anything of ourselves to change our condition. Scarlet doesn't seem to fade. Various colored rags may be thrown on a dump to become victims of the elements: sun, wind, rain. Scarlet remains almost unaffected while other colors fade quickly. (Add some water to show that doing a few good things does not change the sinful condition.) (Rom. 3:20; Titus 3:5)

Only God can cleanse human hearts from the stain and guilt of sin. God invited the people of Judah, who had wandered far from Him into ways of sin, to come to a conference, as it were, to reason with Him about their need for cleansing. "Though your sins are like scarlet, they shall be as white as snow; though they are red like crimson, they shall be like wool" (Is. 1:18). God did the inviting, because only God could do the planning about how to cleanse hearts from sin. God decided to put the guilt and penalty of sin on His own Son. This plan, explained in Isaiah 53, was that God's Son, as the Suffering Servant, would be made an offering for sin. (Compare with Rom. 5:8-9.) (Place the cross into the jar, making sure the vinegar mixes with the "scarlet" liquid.) When a person believes in God's Son and receives Him into his heart, his heart is cleansed in God's sight, "White as snow . . . as wool," twice-cleansed!

God cleanses through the forgiveness of sins, so that we can be saved people, and also that we can find power to live lives that grow in holiness. The power is Christ within us, just as this cross is in the jar. We turn our backs on the very sins we ask forgiveness for. This then means we desire to walk the path of holiness. Rom. 6:22 says that forgiveness results in a life of holiness. The first chapter of Isaiah shows us this too. God's cleansing power puts His forgiven people on a new path: "Wash yourselves; make yourselves clean; remove the evil of your doings from before My eyes; cease to do evil, learn to do good; seek justice, correct oppression" (16-17). We should live in the continual realization that all our sins, even though small in our sight, are as scarlet to God, and that we always need the cleansing through His Son, by the power of His saving cross. As we keep on believing in God's Son as personal Savior, we find His forgiveness a comfort and power every day. Compare Titus 3:4-7. Does your heart respond to God's invitation?

> Whiter than snow, Lord, wash me just now,
> As in Thy presence, humbly I bow.

Read Psalms 51 and 32 with 2 Samuel 11 – 12 in mind about David's sin and cleansing. Read John 4 about the Samaritan woman; Luke 7:36-50 about the sinful woman; Acts 9 about Saul's cleansing; and Luke 24:45-48 about cleansing for the world through the forgiveness of sins.

FAITH THAT OVERCOMES THE WORLD

Materials: Five boxes the same thickness to be used as building blocks. On each box print one of these words: *HATE, TROUBLE, INSECURITY, ANGER, FEAR.* Make a red cardboard cross with rather wide beams, large enough for the lower vertical beam to reach to the top of the blocks. Keep the ends of the blocks even at the beginnings of the words so that when the cross is placed in front of the blocks the word *FAITH* will be seen. Give the blocks to the children ahead of time so they can bring them forward when requested. The first to be placed is the *HATE* block; follow the order in the listing above.

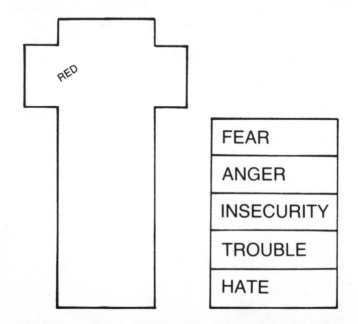

What is it that sets people against people? Why are there wars between the nations? Why is there strife in the home? (Child with HATE comes forward.) It's hate, isn't it? Jesus once said that before He comes again "many will fall away and betray one another and hate one another" (Matt. 24:10). He reminded His followers that they would be hated by the world (Matt. 24:9). So there are many people who build their lives on hate. (James 4:1-2)

There is another building block used by many. Let's see it. It's TROUBLE. Job said in his suffering: "Man is born to trouble as the sparks fly upward" (Job 5:7). There is the trouble of guilt expressed by King David: "My soul is full of troubles" (Ps. 88:3). There is the trouble found in misplaced values: "Trouble befalls the income of the wicked" (Prov. 15:6; compare 1 Tim. 6:9-10). Some people just look for trouble, for they don't seem to find a way out.

What else is wrong in the world? People are insecure. INSECURITY is seen all over, isn't it? It's seen in the anxiety

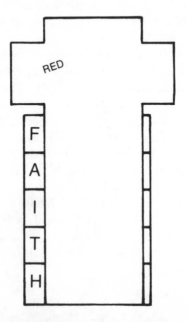

about life. (Matt. 6:31-32). There is worry about the things of life. People try to find meaning by losing themselves in selfish pursuits. The mounting problems in the universe add to the insecurity. (Luke 21:25)

Another problem that plagues the world is ANGER. Anger is an emotion given us by the Creator to be used for self-protection and to fight against evil. But if it falls under the control of the evil in our hearts, it can be overused and misused. Then it is no longer a righteous anger used for good, but it becomes a ruling force in life. Esau was controlled by his anger when he desired to kill Jacob (Gen. 27:45). Cain was angry against Abel (Gen. 4:5-8). Some people are like a match, one scratch and they're off! "A harsh word stirs up anger" (Prov. 15:1). Many people live in anger most of their lives.

To top it all off, people have FEAR. People fear the terrible things happening on earth. "Men fainting with fear and with foreboding of what is coming on the world" (Luke 21:26). The basic problem is the fear of death. The Bible says that the fear of death makes people subject to bondage. (Heb. 2:25)

These blocks are earthly. They are the materials of the human heart by nature. So what is man to do? He can do nothing to rid himself of these evils. These are built-in evils in human life because of sin.

But God has acted in love to rescue the world from these destructive evils. He sent His Son to take the guilt of them away by His death on the cross. (Place red cross in front of the blocks.) Evil fell on Him. He won pardon for the hate, troubles, insecurity, anger, fear, and every other sin in the hearts of men. Isaiah 53 tells us all about this, especially verse 6: "The Lord has laid on Him the iniquity of us all." Through forgiveness God gives a new heart of faith. (Position the cross so that FAITH appears.) Faith is the divinely worked assurance in the believer's heart that Jesus Christ is his personal Savior. Real faith empowers us to rise above these evils of the world and to live above them, just as the horizontal beam of the cross is above these human blocks of evil.

Faith means being born of God. So the apostle John expressed it this way: "Whatever is born of God overcomes the world; and this is the victory that overcomes the world, our faith. Who is it that overcomes the world but he who believes that Jesus is the Son of God?" (1 John 5:4-5; compare 4:10)

If we have faith in Jesus Christ, we need not fear death or anything (Ps. 23:4; 27:1). We need not fear life's problems and trials (Rom. 8:35-39). We have a control for the emotion of anger (Eph. 4:26). We have the security of His loving care (John 10:27-28; Matt. 6:33; Ps. 23:1-3). We have Him as our stronghold in time of trouble (Ps. 9:9; 26:1). We have power to rise above hate feelings (1 John 3:11-14). Jesus spoke to His disciples about the hatred of the world. His words cushion the shock of the world's hatred toward us (John 15:18-19). We stand with Christ, who came through the greatest hate campaign ever as the Conqueror.

Someone said that faith spelled in an acrostic means "Forsaking all, I take Him." So if we forsake all these worldly evils and look to Christ's victory of the cross, that's the practical faith that overcomes the world.

Think of Jeremiah's ministry (Jer. 18:18; 20:1-13; 26:7-16; 38:6-16). David was persecuted by Saul and hunted down by enemies (1 Samuel 18 and 19). A prophet, a king, and many others found the faith that overcomes the world.

FREEDOM IN CHRIST

Materials: A kite. Tie a very thin piece of string to the cord near the kite so that the string breaks with an easy pull.

How many of you children have flown kites? I'm sure most of you have. You experienced real thrills in seeing the kite soar high into the sky. It's fun to feel the tug on the cord, too. What is important when flying your kite? Naturally, it is that you hold tightly to the cord at all times.

Suppose you are flying your kite. (Show how it looks when in flight.) You run it against the wind, and the kite rises into the air. Soon it is above the treetops. Higher and higher it goes. Then it stops rising because you do not give it any more cord. Suppose your kite could talk, and you would hear it say, as it jerked and swayed, "Why does my master hold me back like this? I want to go higher. If my master would cut me loose and set me free, I'd show him how high I could really go." Now let's suppose that the kite in all its pulling and swaying broke the cord (break string with a quick pull) and it went from one side to the other and then took a nosedive. Down it came. It was swept by a wind current right into an electric line. There it was beaten by the wind, until only a few shreads were left. It was not a useful, free kite any longer.

Sometimes we misunderstand what Christian freedom means. To be free in Christ means first of all that He sets us free from the eternal death penalty of our sins. We experience that freedom when we believe in Him as Savior. But in freeing us from sin's penalty, Jesus frees us for service under Him as our new Master. It does not mean we can do whatever we please, any more than this kite is free when the cord is broken. The apostle Paul in his letter to Christians at Galatia warned about misusing Christian liberty. He said: "You were called to freedom, brethren; only do not use your freedom as an opportunity for the flesh, but through love be servants of one another" (Gal. 5:13). This misuse of freedom occurred when the people of Israel were at Mount Sinai awaiting God's law (Exodus 32). God was giving them a law in which they would find freedom of action within the circle of His will. They became impatient when Moses seemed to tarry. They broke themselves loose from God's will and did what they willed. They made their newfound freedom from bondage, which was to be lived within the limits of God's will, a license for the flesh. They were like a kite broken loose. Many of the people died because of the sinful orgy around the idol of the golden calf. They were like the kite beaten to shreads on the electric line. Many people think freedom means to do what they want. They break loose of restraints and do their "thing," becoming addicted to fleshly things and ending up in ruin.

We are free to serve Jesus Christ in love. This means that we make decisions with Him continually. It is very easy to misuse our Christian freedom and make it an occasion for the selfish flesh. As Christians we do not have rule charts in our homes which say, "You must read your Bible two hours each day. You must pray for a half hour each day. You must help with the chores for two hours. You must watch television for only one hour." We don't have such rules, do we? Rather we decide in love for Jesus what to do and when to do it. It's easy to crowd out Bible reading, prayer, and helping at home. Unless we're careful, soon we find no time for the important things. This is misusing our freedom, isn't it? We are letting liberty become a license to serve the old self of sin. Before long, like the kite, we only destroy ourselves. But if we let Jesus hold the cord of our life and decide in love for Him, then we will read our Bibles faithfully, pray regularly, help willingly at home, and do all with love to Jesus.

"What would Jesus do?" is the question that makes up the cord of practical faith. Following Jesus, we can soar high in spiritual joy, peace, and purpose in the service of our Master. He wants to hold the cord of your life always. He died to get that privilege and rose again to make it sure. "For freedom Christ has set us free; stand fast therefore, and do not submit again to a yoke of slavery." (Gal. 5:1)

Christian freedom is in Christ. Outside of Him there is only destruction and eternal death. With Him there is freedom from sin, freedom to serve Him in the power of faith, to be set free from sin's power, until we enjoy perfect freedom in His presence in glory. Jesus said more about this as recorded in John 8:31-32. Think of some Bible people who acted like this kite that wanted to be free. How about Samson (Judges 16) or King David (2 Samuel 11 and 12)? How tangled up their lives became! Christ can untangle the most tangled life.

FRUITFUL LIVING

Materials: Two apples. One apple should be large and red. The other should be unripened and small. Drill a hole in it to resemble a worm hole. If you have a wormy apple for the second apple, then cut it to show the damage.

Almost everyone enjoys an apple like this one. Isn't it a beauty? Someone has said that you can enjoy an apple with all five senses. You can see its color, smell its fragrance, feel its firmness, hear its crispy crunch, and taste its juicy flavor.

But here is another apple. Look it over. What difference do you observe between this one and the red one? Size? Color? Someone is saying, "I see a worm hole." What's worse than a worm in an apple? It's half a worm! Which of these would you like to eat?

The problem with the second apple is the worm. The worm retarded the growth of the apple and made it unusable. Where do apple worms come from? One boy imagined that they come down the road looking for apple trees with nice juicy apples on them. They crawl up the tree and into an apple and then eat all they want. But that is not the truth, is it? Most often a codling moth lays its eggs in the blossom. When the eggs hatch, the larvae find themselves in the very center of the tiny apple. They destroy the apple's heart. In a spiritual way it all goes back to the fall into sin by the first parents of our human race. The devil like a codling moth brought the "eggs" of evil. Our first parents sinned, and this put evil in every heart. "Sin came into the world through one man and death through sin, and so death spread to all men because all men sinned" (Rom. 5:12). It happened at the blossom time of creation.

The "eggs" of evil must be dealt with early in each blossom to prevent them from hatching and taking over the life of the apple. God has given the remedy. "The free gift in the grace of that one man Jesus Christ abounded for many" (Rom. 5:15). God has a way of applying this grace at blossom time to young hearts. It is the application of the water of Baptism. "Be baptized, every one of you, in the name of Jesus Christ for the forgiveness of your sins . . . . For the promise is to you and to your children" (Acts 2:38-39). This is spelled out in Titus 3:4-7. Some use chemical spray, some use plain water for apple-blossom spray. Spiritually, there is one remedy. It's the grace of God in Christ that produces the new birth of faith and new life in the Spirit. The Spirit-life is nurtured by the Word of God, just as a tree needs proper nurture to produce juicy, red apples.

The apostle Paul lists many evil things that are like (railroad) worms that ruin an apple: "Immorality, impurity, licentiousness, idolatry, . . . anger, selfishness, dissension, party spirit, envy, drunkenness, carousing" (Gal. 5:19-21). He calls them works of the flesh. The devil's wormy apples do not get gathered into God's garner. They are fit for the garbage can of eternal death! People who love to keep on doing the works of the flesh do not inherit the kingdom of God.

The apostle also lists the fruits of the Spirit. These are the beautiful things that belong to the life in Christ. They are "love, joy, peace, patience, kindness, goodness, faithfulness, gentleness, self-control" (Gal. 5:22-23). "If we live by the Spirit, let us also walk by the Spirit." (Gal. 5:25)

Be thankful if you had the early application of God's grace by Baptism and the hearing of it in God's Word. Remember every day that you are the special object of God's love, and He wants you to be like a beautiful, red apple. We look at this apple and say, "What a wonderful Creator God is!" People look at your beautiful living, and "they . . . see your good works and give glory to your Father who is in heaven." (Matt. 5:16)

Does anyone know the name of this apple? (Be sure you know it). God has provided a variety of apples. So He has a large variety of His own people who enjoy fruitful living. Best of all, God has our names written in heaven. (Luke 10:20)

Think about some examples from the Bible on this subject. There was Lot and his family who lived in the city called Sodom which was full of "wormy apples." God rescued Lot and his family (Genesis 19). Noah and his family were God's "red apples" in the days of the Great Deluge (Genesis 6 to 8). Elijah and the false prophets of Baal show us the contrast too (1 Kings 16:29 – 18:46). We are to aim at living apart from the ungodly. Final separation will take place on Judgment Day. (2 Peter 2 – 3; 1 Cor. 5:9-13; Rev. 21:22-27; 22:10-15; and the Letter of Jude)

The miracle-working power of God's grace is so great that He can take a "wormy apple" like Paul and transform him later in life into a beautiful life. But think of all those years of beautiful living he missed! Let us show in our living that we are thankful for God's grace that makes our lives fruitful from childhood.

GOD IN THREE PERSONS

Materials: A prescription bottle for a child.

Do you know what kind of bottle I have in my hand? Yes, it's a prescription bottle. On its label I notice that the medicine was prescribed for a child.

I want you to think about how many persons were involved in getting this medicine to the ill child. Who made the diagnosis of the child's illness and then prescribed the right medicine? It was the doctor, the family physician. Who filled the prescription? It was the pharmacist at the drug store. With great knowledge, skill, and care, he put in the right ingredients. Who gave the child the medicine? It was mother or father, who followed the directions carefully. They faithfully stood by the child and administered the medicine with a lot of love. The child got well.

This reminds us how God is active toward us. He is one God in His being, yet three in His Persons. As God in three Persons, He acts to cure us of our sin-sickness. God the Father diagnosed the illness of the world and wrote the prescription. "None is righteous, no, not one; no one understands, no one seeks for God. All have turned aside, together they have gone wrong; no one does good, not even one. . . . There is no distinction; since all have sinned and fall short of the glory of God, they are justified by His grace as a gift, through the redemption which is in Christ Jesus, whom God put forward as an expiation by His blood, to be received by faith" (Rom. 3:10-12, 22-25). God the Father is the doctor or family physician of the world.

God the Son came in the fullness of time. He was born of a human mother to take on the human nature of flesh and blood. He offered His sinless life on the cross to pay for the eternal death penalty of sin. This involved the shedding of His holy, precious blood. His blood was the saving ingredient. It says in 1 Peter that you were ransomed "with the precious blood of Christ, like that of a lamb without blemish or spot" (1:19). God the Son is the dedicated pharmacist who fills the prescription, fills it with His own lifeblood.

God the Holy Spirit gives us the medicine. He is our Comforter and Counselor who stands at our side and convinces us of our need for God's healing remedy in the blood of Christ. He gives us the medicine by working faith in us, for "no one can say 'Jesus is Lord' except by the Holy Spirit" (1 Cor. 12:3). Jesus promised: "I will pray the Father, and He will give you another Counselor, to be with you forever, even the Spirit of truth . . . for He dwells with you and will be in you." (John 14:16-17)

When we take the "medicine" by real faith we get well. We pass from spiritual death to spiritual life (John 5:24). This is a miracle. It is a new birth. Besides, it doesn't cost us anything. Think how much it costs to fill prescriptions! The Son of God does it freely. "The free gift of God is eternal life in Christ Jesus our Lord." (Rom. 6:23)

The fact that each Person of God is fully God, and yet there are not three Gods, is a mystery to us. Nevertheless God is what He says He is. Let us praise Him for being active in His three Persons to effect our new birth and our spiritual healing. "By this we know that we abide in Him and He in us, because He has given us of His own Spirit. And we have seen and testify that the Father has sent His Son as the Savior of the world." (1 John 4:13-14)

Read about Nicodemus, John 3:1-16. He felt something

was wrong. He came to Jesus. He had a hard time going along with the diagnosis and prescription. He came for instruction, but needed salvation. He came to a teacher, but found his Savior. He put a lot of stock in head knowledge, but found heart regeneration. He found a perfect cure with God's medicine.

The matter of being spiritually healed means that we all become as little children. We humbly take the medicine. God in three Persons does the healing. We do not reject the medicine just because we don't understand the mystery of the Trinity (that's three-in-one God) any more than we reject the medicine just because we don't have the mind of the doctor, or the training of the pharmacist, or the experience of a parent.

Read Psalm 103; Eph. 1:3-14; Rom. 5:1-11; Is. 48: 16-17; Matt. 3:16-17 to enlarge on the idea of God's healing love expressed in "God in three Persons, blessed Trinity."

GOD LOVES THE WORLD

Materials: Four types of shoes or sandals: for baby, child, man, and woman. The shoes should be in four colors: red, yellow, black, and white.

(Display the man's shoe.) What are shoes for? They are to protect our feet when we go places, aren't they? They are not exactly worn for comfort. Right now we might feel more comfortable if we could take our shoes off! But we wear them and put up with discomfort to have protection wherever we walk. So in a spiritual way shoes remind us of Jesus' command: "Go into all the world and preach the Gospel to the whole creation." (Mark 16:15)

(Display the baby shoe with the man's shoe.) What do these two shoes together suggest? Surely they suggest growth. Much food and exercise went between the baby-size shoe and the adult size. As Christians we are to grow. "Grow in the grace and knowledge of our Lord and Savior Jesus Christ" (2 Peter 3:18). We are to grow in maturity: "Speaking the truth in love, we are to grow up in every way into Him who is the head, into Christ." (Eph. 4:15)

(Display all four shoes.) What do these four shoes remind us of in a spiritual way? We think of the central truth of the Bible, don't we? That truth is that God loves the whole world (John 3:16). This is put in a children's hymn in these words:

> Red and yellow, black and white,
> They are precious in His sight.

Shoes tell us a lot about a person, don't they? Suppose a person is walking through a doorway and you are watching from the side. Without seeing the person's face you would know from the shoes whether the person is a child or adult, male or female. Also shoes may say something about a person's habits. If shoes are neat and shiny, it shows tidiness. Shoes indicate at times the occupation of a person. Shoes remind us that how we live is very important. People are watching. "Now you are light in the Lord; walk as children of light" (Eph. 5:8). "Blessed is the man who walks not in the counsel of the wicked . . . but his delight is in the law of the Lord" (Ps. 1:1-2). We might call this glowing for God.

We are to be going, growing, glowing Christians. Yet sometimes we forget our calling to share God's love with the world. We act like a stubborn, confused Jonah! God told him to go to Nineveh with the message of God's love. Instead he tried to flee from God and to avoid going. He was told to go east, and he went west instead! (Tell the account of Jonah's experience in the sea monster's belly, his prayer of repentance, and his being given a second chance to go and tell, chapters 1 to 3 of Jonah.) Even after Jonah went and told, and the people repented, Jonah was not happy. He sat on the east side of the city under a booth and moped and prayed to die. He complained to God: "That is why I made haste to flee to Tarshish; for I knew that Thou art a gracious God and merciful, slow to anger, and abounding in steadfast love" (Jonah 4:2). Jonah, like many of his countrymen, didn't take the universal love of God seriously. They sort of boxed up God's love and labeled it "For Jews only." Jonah admitted that he just could not stand the idea of God being forgiving to his country's enemies. Jonah did not willingly go with the story of God's love, because he did not grow in the knowledge of God's love for the world, and his life did little glowing as he moped in his little booth. But we can understand from the rest of chapter 4, as God tenderly instructed Jonah, that Jonah did a lot of growing and was glad to go and glow for God.

We should be always willing to share the story of God's love with the world. God sent His only Son to become a human to redeem the world. He was like us in all respects, only sinless. During the thirty-three years on earth He wore baby shoes, child's shoes, and man's shoes as He walked our sin-weary earth in the interest of its salvation. He walked to Calvary's cross to give His life as a payment for the world's sins. When we believe in Him personally, then love for Him and thanksgiving to Him will move us to go and grow and glow for God. (See Jonah 2:9; 2 Cor. 5:17-21)

GOD'S FORBEARING LOVE

Materials: The letter *H* made of paper, the size you desire. One side should be red, the other gold. The crossbar should be somewhat above center. The sides are folded inward so that they overlap. This will make a cross. Begin with the red to the outside. You will need a piece of metal or wood to reinforce the cross on the vertical beam. You will need a red rubber band. Your hand will be involved as part of the demonstration.

Think about this rubber band for a moment. Just as surely as you know it will break if I stretch it too far (stretch it quite a distance, but do not break it), so the Bible says that Jesus will come again on Judgment Day. "You yourselves know well that the day of the Lord will come like a thief in the night" (1 Thess. 5:2). Yet I can stretch this rubber band quite a bit before it will break. God in a way has stretched His patience much more than this rubber band is stretched. He does this so that more time is given for people to come to repentance. Peter informs us: "The Lord is not slow about His promise as some count slowness, but is forbearing toward you, not wishing that any should perish, but that all should reach repentance. But the day of the Lord will come like a thief." (2 Peter 3:9-10)

The Lord has delayed coming for judgment for almost two thousand years. The reason is clear. It's because of the great redemption won by Jesus Christ on the cross. God's redeeming love goes out from the cross (1 Cor. 1:18). (Pull the rubber band with your hand in both directions, covering both the Old and the New Testament.) People in the Old Testament looked forward to God's redeeming love in Christ. New Testament people look backward to the cross-event (Luke 24:44-48; Rom. 3:21-24). God's plan is to draw as many as possible to the saving cross of His Son. He gave His Son in so much love that there is forgiveness for every sinner in the world. God wants to save all people, but some are lost by their own fault. (For the above, anchor the rubber band to the cross.)

Look again at the rubber band. What color is it? Red. What does this suggest? It reminds us that those who come to the Father by Jesus Christ are saved by His blood (1 John 1:7). When people find forgiveness through the Gospel of God's love, this is called the time of grace. Until Judgment Day God urgently invites: "Behold, now is the acceptable time; behold, now is the day of salvation" (2 Cor. 6:2). This rubber band can be stretched to surround larger and larger bundles. Right now all the fingers of my hand and my thumb are within the pull of the rubber band. So God's people are added to the church and kept in the body of Christ by daily repentance.

Another thing about God's forbearing love is that it reaches out to the straying and draws them back with steadfast love. (Show how the tension increases when one of your fingers pulls outward.) That love brought Peter to repentance (Luke 22:61-62). It brought king David back (2 Sam. 12:13). See Luke 15 for illustrations of the steadfast love of God.

The rubber band is round. This reminds us of eternity. God has eternity in mind when He loves. He does not want people to be separated from Him eternally, so He gave His Son to die as the penalty for sin on the cross in the place of sinful people. He loves so that we may have eternal life. (John 3:36)

When the last person to be saved is saved, then the Lord will come for judgment. (Stretch rubber band until it breaks.) The day of grace will be over at that time. There will be no more opportunity for repentance. The call of the cross will be completed. Those who believed will receive eternal life with resurrected bodies of glory (John 5:29; Phil. 3:20; 1 John 3:2-3). Unbelievers will have to depart to eternal remorse and shame (Matt. 25:46). The public verdict on Judgment Day will be based on what people did with the Gospel in their lifetime (Rom. 2:16). Faith saves. Unbelief condemns. Another way the Bible presents the Judgment Day event is by pointing out what is visible about faith or unbelief. Deeds of love prove faith, by which alone a person is saved. Lack of faith is shown by lack of deeds of love. (James 2:17; Eph. 2:8-10; John 5:29; Matt. 25: 31-46)

(Show the golden letter *H*.) When Jesus comes in glory for judgment, He will prepare new heavens and a new earth. This will be the new order of things where believers will be blessed in the heaven of God. Our commonwealth is in heaven (Phil. 3:20). Our names are written there (Luke 10:20). Our hope is laid up there (Col. 1:5). It is reserved for us (1 Peter 1:4). It is pictured as the golden city of eternal security (Rev. 21:10, 18). The old order of things will pass away (2 Peter 3:3-15). The new order will be free of sin and perfect with righteousness.

(Make a circle with the *H*.) Place your hand, which represented believers in the kingdom of grace, within the circle. Heaven is being with the Lord forever and being perfected into His likeness. (Ps. 17:15) Until that time, let us be found in true faith in Jesus Christ as our personal Savior.

Daniel 12 and 1 Thess. 5:1-11 give us more information on our Lord's second coming.

GROWING IN THE GRACE OF GIVING

Materials: Ten apples and an apple core. One of the apples should be smaller; another should be small and green. (You may substitute other commodities like potatoes or oranges or whatever tells the story best for your area. If you substitute, then a peeling will replace the apple core in the demonstration.) Display the apples in a box for all to see. You will need a gray heart almost large enough to cover the apples, a red cross the size of the box, and a white heart the size of the gray one. You will also need a knife to cut the apple.

Here are ten red, juicy apples. These may represent the gifts that God gives to us to sustain our lives. We have nothing of ourselves. God is the Giver of all. The apples are applied to maintaining our daily lives to procure food, shelter, clothing, education, recreation, taxes, payments, and the like. That takes care of about nine apples. Children and young people who do not yet have a salary are involved in the gifts of God in the family structure.

There is one apple left. God says, "Give Me an apple (or two) as a 'thank you' for the other apples." This apple should be applied to gifts for His kingdom. But does everyone do it? The hearts of all human beings are selfish by nature. (Place the gray heart over the apples.) The natural desire is to use the tenth apple for self and even grumble over why there aren't more.

God is a generous giver. He makes it possible for people to give. God gave something else of more importance. He gave His only Son to be a sin-offering. He paid for the guilt of selfish hearts. (Place the red cross over the gray heart.) When a person believes in God's Son, God gives again. He gives a new heart by the Holy Spirit. (Place white heart over the gray heart.) The new heart is alive in the Spirit and has various spiritual virtues, including gratitude. Thus, a born-again believer has the inner power to thank God through Jesus Christ.

The apostle Paul wrote: "You know the grace of our Lord Jesus Christ, that though He was rich, yet for your sake He became poor, so that by His poverty you might become rich" (2 Cor. 8:9). We must remember that God's eternal Son became really poor for us. He was born in a cattle shed, laid in a manger, worked as a carpenter, traveled about during His ministry with no place to lay His head. He chose to die the shameful death of the cross. This poverty led Him to taste eternal death for every person. He experienced every sinner's God-forsakenness in all its terror and darkness. So for believers there is favor with God, peace, and joy. Life is rich with spiritual life that never ends.

As we realize this, we begin to realize that giving is a great privilege. There is no law that says how much we are to give. Love determines the amount. It could be that there are times when the apples (our gifts) are small. (Show the small green apple.) This could be in the time of childhood. Perhaps as a child you get a small allowance or have very small earnings. Perhaps as a youth you have but a part-time job and a lot of expenses for education. (Show the other smaller apple.) Or there are times when employees are laid off, or when business is not so good, or when crops fail, or when the salary is reduced to a smaller retirement pay. What then? Then you can give only of the small apples. The Bible allows for this. "On the first day of every week each of you is to put something aside and store it up, as he may prosper" (1 Cor. 16:2). The main thing is that gifts are the firstfruits type and given regularly.

Also, if the apples are small and the needs are great at certain times, it may be necessary to cut the tenth apple. If you cut it in half, that makes you a five-percent giver. If you cut off a quarter, that makes you a two-and-one-half percent giver. Before cutting it like that, let's remember the cross. What a sacrifice God's Son made! What a gift God gave! But, sadly, it happens. People let the old nature of greed regulate their giving. (Expose the gray heart some.) When the old nature interferes with giving, then self finally eats the tenth apple, and God gets the core. (Show the browned core.) This is fit for the garbage! Such giving is called token giving. Surely that type of giving does not fit with the cross and the new heart and the blessings of ten nice apples, does it?

There is a secret for giving that should be the secret of our lives. The apostle reveals it in 2 Cor. 8:1-9. The secret is God's grace. Grace is His love to undeserving sinners. The secret really was evident in the actions of Christians of Macedonia. These people had financial set-backs. Extreme poverty! Many of their apples were small and green. Yet they gave God from the bigger ones: "Their abundance of joy and their extreme poverty have over-flowed in a wealth of liberality on their part." Now another secret. "First they gave themselves to the Lord and to us by the will of God." They were rich in heart. First the heart must be given to God. The apostle adds: "Now as you excell in everything—in faith, in utterance, in knowledge, in all earnestness, and in your love for us—see that you excel in this gracious work also" (2 Cor. 8:7). "The render-ing of this service not only supplies the wants of the saints but also overflows in many thanksgivings to God." (2 Cor. 9:12; read the entire section, 6-15)

71

Small gifts receive God's blessing when given in love. The widow gave a small gift of two mites (Mark 12:41-44). God is first interested in the quality of the gift, that is, whether the heart is in the giving. Then He is interested in the quantity. Amounts follow love. The widow first gave herself.

Are you growing in the grace of giving? Do you give regularly? Do you give from the heart? Do you give first-fruits, from the top of your income? Do you give generously? Woe to us if we are not poor widows and give but two mites! (Compare Mal. 1:6-14; 3:8-12 on what the Old Testament says about giving.) (Compare also Ex. 35:4-28, the gifts for the tabernacle.)

HANDLE WITH PRAYER

Materials: Some incense and a container in which to burn it, a plaque or picture of the praying hands, and a standing cross large enough to be seen behind the plaque.

(Light the incense.) You might be wondering what we can learn from seeing smoke rise. Our thoughts are to go back to a reference in Ex. 40:5 where God prescribed that incense be burned at prayer time in Israel's worship. The psalmist later speaks of it, saying: "Let my prayers be counted as incense before Thee" (Ps. 141:2). Zechariah was praying at the time of incense (Luke 1:9-10). The smoke of incense is a meaningful symbol of prayer. Smoke that rises from burning materials usually diffuses. But the smoke of incense rises like a stream. This reminds us that God indeed hears the prayers of His people. As surely as smoke rises upward, so believers have the guarantee that God hears their prayers. Every believer has to know this before he will open up and talk heart to heart with God. The idea of incense is further expressed in Rev. 8:3-4 in connection with the prayers of the saints. The first thing about prayer is to be assured that God hears (Is. 65:24; Luke 11:5-13). God hears even the sighs of our hearts for help, praise, and thanksgiving. Because God hears, we are given a "hot line" to God so we may handle everything with prayer. (Phil. 4:6)

(Place the symbol of the praying hands behind the incense.) What attitude is expressed by the praying hands?

73

It is the attitude of surrender, isn't it? The same idea is expressed in folded hands. It is saying, "I surrender to Your will, Lord." Or, "Handcuff me, Lord." Prayer power comes when we want God's will to take us captive. It is possible to surrender only as we realize what real prayer is. Real prayer is faith that talks with God. Faith is worked in our hearts and kept glowing by the presence of the Holy Spirit in our hearts. Since God has moved into our hearts by the Holy Spirit, it stands to reason that God's thoughts, desires, attitudes, holiness must saturate our being. Jesus Himself prayed that way with power (Luke 22:42). The apostle John caught that idea and shared his experience in prayer: "This is the confidence which we have in Him, that if we ask anything according to His will, He hears us" (1 John 5:14). God would be a monster to be feared rather than our Father to be trusted if He acted in plain power apart from His will of eternal love and gave us every selfish wish on our part. So in prayer we talk everything over with God and leave everything to His will, which is wiser than our own. We are willing to accept any answer: "Yes, no, wait, I wish to substitute." All the while we are enjoying peace of heart in knowing that if God knows, all is well. God's will for us is that we be saved, sanctified, and patient in life's sufferings. (1 Tim. 2:4; 1 Thess. 4:3; Acts 14:22). His will is for our eternal good. Who wouldn't "give himself up" to God's will and handle life with prayer?

(Place the cross behind the incense and praying hands.) Another part of real prayer is symbolized by the cross. Jesus said: "Truly, truly, I say to you, if you ask anything of the Father, He will give it to you in My name" (John 16:23). The name Jesus is not some magic letter set to get God moving to serve our selfish desires. Rather it is the name that is equated with the work of redeeming the world. God hears prayers of sinners, as imperfect as their prayers are, just because of the redeeming work of Jesus. God can forgive sins and give His Holy Spirit because of the redeeming work of Jesus on the cross. So prayer power comes when our conversations with God are conditioned by Jesus' name. God gives the gifts that befit a child of His who is redeemed by Jesus. The name of Jesus moves us to seek the Giver more than the gift. We desire the "cross things" first. We trust that God will add all we need for a meaningful Christian life. (Matt. 6:33)

Every problem, trial, trouble, sorrow, as well as every joy, success, thanksgiving, and praise should be handled with prayer. The Spirit of God gets us through (Rom. 8:26-27). Abraham prayed before he rescued Lot (Gen. 18:16-19; chap. 29). Hannah prayed for a son (1 Sam. 1:9-18). Hezekiah prayed for longer life (2 Kings 19:14-20; 20:1-7). The disciples prayed and were filled with the Spirit (Acts 1:12-14; 2:1-4). The early Christians prayed for Peter's deliverance (Acts 12:1-17). Cornelius prayed to hear the pure Gospel preached (Acts 10:1-48). Do you handle everything with prayer? God answers every prayer, either by giving what we ask or something better.

HANDS OF BLESSING

Materials: Your hands. Demonstrate the points in the lessons with your hands.

What a wonderful gift of God our hands are! God thought of everything when He made hands, didn't He? He did not stick the hands on the sides of the body like stubs or flippers. (Demonstrate how difficult it would be to shake a hand or pick up anything.) God put the hands on giant swivels that turn in all directions. He did not put one finger or only a thumb on our hands, for that would make our hands like pokers. They would be more dangerous than helpful. Rather God made them with many-jointed fingers (four) and a thumb. Our hands can hold handles, throw balls, use eating utensils. Our hands are blessed with many skills. They have a delicate sense of touch. They are symbols of bodily powers, the expression of inner desires, the projection of the human personality, and indications of a person's vocation. Hands are not masters, only servants. They do what our mind orders them to do. If we desire evil, hands respond to evil; if good, they do good. So it all has to do with the renewing of our minds (Rom. 12:1-2). Let us make some Bible observations in connection with our hands being the expression of inner desires. How are we to live as Christians?

Our hands are to be praying hands. Peter writes: "The end of all things is at hand; therefore keep sane and sober for your prayers" (1 Peter 4:7). Timothy heard from the apostle Paul: "I desire then that in every place the men should pray, lifting holy hands without anger or quarreling" (1 Tim. 2:8). Folded hands indicate surrender to God's will. It's like saying, "Handcuff me, God, with Your will." In olden times surrender in prayer was symbolized by holding up the hands in an "I-give-up manner." Either way, our life as Christians should be given to prayer. There is so much wrong in this world and there are so many failings in our lives that we could merely wring our hands in disgust. Some go so far as to clench their hands in fists of defiance against God. They see all the evil in the world and say, "If there is a God, why doesn't He do something about it?" (Luke 21:26; 2 Peter 3:1-7; 2 Tim. 3:1-5). But as Christians we can talk to God about everything. We know that God's love in Christ is so strong that nothing can separate us from that love. We can say: "God, make me bold to do Your will. Where there is dishonesty, help me be honest. Where there is hate, help me show love. Where there is cheating, help me be truthful. Help me trust and act in the assurance that You have the whole world under control, no matter how it might look sometimes in the morning paper."

Our hands should be hands extended in handclasps, or handshakes, of love. "Above all hold unfailing love for one another, since love covers a multitude of sins" (1 Peter 4:8). Our hands could easily be used as pointers. We could point out the faults of others and conduct a real smear campaign. In this way we could show off our goodness alongside the faults of others. But we know better, don't we? Look at the hand that's a pointer. When I point a finger at someone, three point back at me. I know I have faults too. God for Jesus' sake forgives me my faults. I can afford to overlook them in others and cover them from the view of others by saying only good things of others. That's putting forth the handclasp of love. Our homes, Sunday school classes, churches, community organizations, and schools can operate smoothly only when there is genuine love.

Our hands should be open hands. Open hands are sharing hands, or serving hands. Peter writes: "Practice hospitality . . . . As each has received a gift, employ it for one another as good stewards of God's varied grace" (1 Peter 4:9-10). Our hands could easily become clenched hands in selfishness, serving only self. If our hearts are greedy, then our hands will be clenched, and we will live with the "never enough" attitude. If we have hearts that realize we are here to share God's love and gifts, we will dedicate our self, service, and substance to God, saying, "Take my hands and let them move At the impulse of Thy love." We do whatever we can to share God's saving grace with others. Each of us should realize that Christ has no hands to give out the Bread of life but mine.

Our hands are to be working hands. We could sit on our hands, or let them hang down in idleness. The apostle Paul says: "Labor, doing honest work with his hands, so that he may be able to give to those in need" (Eph. 4:28). (Compare 2 Thess. 3:6-13.) As children you attend school. You are using your hands to hold pencils in learning. You work with your hands to prepare for future work with your hands. You work with your hands to care for your body. You help around home. All this because you believe that God has saved you to serve Him. "Whatever your hand finds to do, do it with your might" (Eccl. 9:10). Ps. 90:16-17 is a fitting prayer that God would give us hands of blessing: "Yea, the work of our hands establish Thou it."

Read about Abraham, who shared, Gen. 14:17-24; the Wise Men, Matt. 2:11; Zacchaeus, Luke 19:1-10; Elisha and the Shunammite, 2 Kings 4; David's kindness to Mephibosheth, 2 Samuel 9.

HOLY COMMUNION
AND CHRISTIAN CROSSBEARING

Materials: A white paper in 4″ by 12″ proportion. Make as large as you desire. Accordion-fold to make 13 folds. Color the back side of the last fold gray. The bottom half will become the Communion table. From the top half cut a cross, leaving the hinges intact. When unfolded there are 13 crosses to depict the scene around the table in the Upper Room. The last cross on the right is for Judas, who betrayed Jesus. The cross is to be cut from the fellowship of faith, which is represented by the joined crosses. The cut cross is bent downward to show that Judas fell from "faith." The gray represents his eternal perdition. This is to be done during the lesson. Do the folding of the paper ahead of time. Have a pair of scissors handy, also a red marking pencil.

Jesus told His disciples: "If any man would come after Me, let him deny himself and take up his cross and follow Me" (Matt. 16:24). I shall cut this piece of folded paper to make a cross. As I open it, you can see a number of crosses. What Bible scene does this suggest? Indeed, it is the Upper Room scene where the first Holy Communion was given. The bottom part of this paper represents the table. The crosses depict Jesus and His disciples. In the case of Jesus we can understand why. But crosses for disciples? Let's keep in mind what Jesus said, "Take up his cross and follow Me."

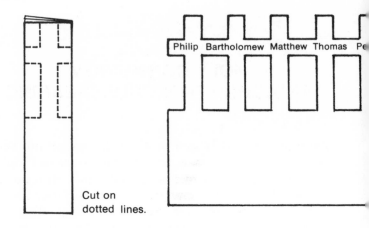

Philip Bartholomew Matthew Thomas Pe...

Cut on
dotted lines.

Let us identify Jesus' cross at the table by marking it
with five wounds in red. The very next day Jesus went to
present Himself on the high altar of Calvary as the Lamb
of God that takes away the sin of the world. Blood came
out of His hands, feet, and side.

Jesus gave much instruction at that table (John 13 to
17). He also pointed out who would betray Him. It was
Judas. (Cut the hinge of the horizontal beam on the right
cross and bend it downward.) Judas lost the faith he perhaps had and fell victim to eternal death, which is represented by gray, the darkness of his night of despair as the
son of perdition (John 17:12). (Cut off the Judas' cross and
throw it aside.) Judas died a miserable death by taking his
own life.

After Judas left, Jesus took some of the bread and wine
of the Passover meal and blessed them, saying: "Take, eat;
this is My body. . . . Drink of it . . . this is My blood of the
covenant . . . for the forgiveness of sins" (Matt. 26:26-28).
Compare accounts in Luke 22, Mark 14, and 1 Corinthians
11. Jesus made a special presence of Himself possible in

80

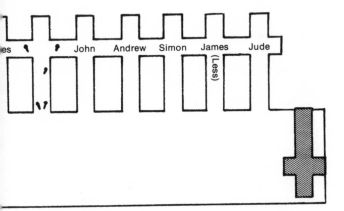

es   John   Andrew   Simon   James   Jude
(Less)

this institution. It was His way of sharing His presence with needy disciples to the end of time. A good term for that is "Real Presence." Jesus shares Himself in a supernatural way in the eating of the bread and drinking of the wine in Holy Communion. The white crosses stand for the fact that the disciples were believers in Christ, cleansed by the Word (John 15:3) and thus made worthy of Holy Communion.

Holy Communion is for saved people – to empower them to grow in faith and sanctified living. His closeness of love makes that possible. The disciples felt quite capable of coping with life's problems when Jesus was in their midst. When He said He was returning to His Father (by way of the cross and open tomb), they were saddened and perplexed. But in Holy Communion Jesus gave them the gift of Himself, to be within each of them, not just around them. He would go with them and every disciple who communes to the end of time. So Holy Communion is special comfort, a strengthening by the living presence of Jesus. The table is white to remind us that every Communion is a joyous

81

celebration of Jesus' presence within. "My Savior dwells within my heart: How blest am I! How good Thou art!" (*The Lutheran Hymnal*, 309)

The disciples are depicted by crosses as a reminder of the fact that to be real disciples much self-denial is necessary. Jesus called self-denial a cross. It is painful to say no to the cravings of our evil nature. We must say no to allurements of the world, no to the enticements of the devil, who travels as an angel of light. Saying no is very painful and is called crucifying the flesh. Each time we say no we are driving a nail into sinful self. That hurts. To do that we need the power and the presence of Jesus. We need to experience His love to put up with the cross of self-denial. The realization that "Jesus is with me" determines our course of action when we ask, "What does Jesus want me to do?" This realization receives new life every time we partake of Communion.

Let us get better acquainted with the disciples to see how Holy Communion helped them grow in grace. (It is good to know them by name. An easy way to remember the names is to group them in fours according to their initials: P-J-J-A, P-B-M-T, and S-J-J-J. That's Peter, James, John, and Andrew, two sets of brothers. Next, Philip, Bartholomew, Matthew, Thomas. Then Simon, James the Less, Jude, and Judas Iscariot.) Let's position them at the table with Jesus by initialing the crosses. Closest to Jesus was John, the cross on the right of Jesus' cross. James on the other side of Jesus. Then Peter and Andrew next to James and John. The four crosses on the left for P-B-M-T. Those on the right for S and the 3 Js. Judas' cross is gone. (See Matt. 10:2-4; Mark 3:16-19; Luke 6:14-16.)

The disciples had weaknesses! If Holy Communion were a perfection banquet for the pious in life, no one else could ever commune. Communion is to help weak disciples grow in grace. Peter was self-reliant, impulsive, self-confident. He even denied Jesus that very night. So weak! But Peter remembered! He did grow strong (read his epistles). James and John were argumentive, selfish, "sons of thunder," because their souls rumbled with impatience. John grew in love. He went all the way with Jesus to the cross. Read his epistles as the apostle of love. James became an early martyr. Thomas had a gloomy, doubting nature. Later he said, "My Lord and my God." Philip lacked vision. He tried to be so scientific about faith (John 6:5-7). He learned better. Simon the Zealot had seared his soul by the fires of hate that burned out of control so long. He was sanctified for service to Jesus. Each disciple had a lot of saying no to old ways and fleshly cravings. They had new power to say it, and they did. These men revolutionized their world.

Another look at those crosses around the first table. They are joined in oneness. One with Jesus, one with each other. They found added strength in the bond of faith. Instead of judging, there was love and acceptance. They had power to bear with each other's infirmities in the love of Christ. Instead of Simon sitting there thinking about Matthew's sins, he accepted him in love of Jesus, and together they followed Jesus in service. It works that way with all who commune and remember, out where the action is, that Jesus is in their very hearts. Rifts between spouses, parents and teen-agers, children and parents, and between church members are healed in Communion. Each one receives inner strength for victorious crossbearing, for a closer walk with Christ. (1 Cor. 10:16-17)

HOMES FOR HEAVEN

Materials: A pair of scissors. A letter *H* made from 8½″ by 11″ white paper and a sheet of paper the same size. The *H* will first be used as a pattern. Then one of the *H* letters will be folded to form a cross. The outside bars are folded toward the center so as to make one bar. Be sure that the crossbar of the *H* is somewhat above center so that a cross can be formed.

(Display the letter *H*.) Suppose you were told to make a letter exactly like this one. What would you do? First you get a piece of paper large enough. Then you get the scissors. If you are a careless person, you might begin cutting just from looks, or for that matter, if you are careless enough, you might just tear it without even using the scissors. But remember that I said, "Suppose you were told to make a letter exactly like this one." Thus you hold the *H* as a pattern, even clip it on, and cut carefully, and you have a letter *H* exactly like this one. We will let the letter stand for that important institution which makes our churches and our country strong. You guessed it. It is home.

Now we will focus our attention on the pair of scissors. The scissors will stand for the partners that make the home. The scissors cut out the *H* as both of the blades worked together. If the partners forget about their common goal, if one or the other refuses to work toward that goal, then the building of the home is very difficult, and it is not very successful. Sadly, some marriages are separated by the forces of evil. Imagine the problem you would have around the house if every time you wanted to use the scissors you found them separated—the blades in different places, the screw in another. Then you would have to insert the screw, and with a screwdriver make sure to tighten it just right! It is best when the scissors are joined and tightened right and left in the proper place for regular use. The scissors thus joined stand for unity in marriage. In fact, as these blades work together, they often form a cross (show the shape of the plus, or Greek ✚ cross). The presence, power, and peace of Christ is the "plus" that gives marriage unity and goal.

Another thing about the scissors. For successful cutting the blades have to match, to the very point. Can you imagine the difficulty if one blade were of a different make and size! There are important things to look for when looking for a partner in life to help build the home. It is important to look for good manners, good habits, the qualities of honesty, integrity, industry, and the like. Yet there is something more important for marital success. It is the bond of common faith in Christ with an active interest in practicing the Christian way of life. When one of the partners is not a Christian, or is lax about the faith, trouble is bound to come. The home then is not built according to God's plan. God's plan is that the home is to be a church in miniature, a stepping-stone to glory. It is a nursery of heaven where children are brought to Jesus in Baptism by loving parents and first learn about Jesus (Eph. 6:4; Titus 3:4-7). The home is where partners help each other grow in grace and in the hope of heaven by sharing God's Word daily and richly. (Fold *H* to make a cross.) The blessings of His cross are forgiveness and peace and the hope of heaven. When you grow up and look for a partner in life, be sure to look for unity in the faith. (Eph. 4:1-6; 2 Cor. 6:14-18)

H reminds us of another home. What is it? Indeed, the home of heaven. People who are born anew are born for heaven (Eph. 1:3-10). New-birth people need the nurture of God's Word of grace, and this is best done in the setting of a Christian home where God's grace is shared in word and deed. The blades of the scissors must face each other as they work together. Even so partners are able to face up to each other and admit when they have done wrong and ask for forgiveness and forgive. Someone has said that a successful marriage is made up of happy forgivers.

A few more thoughts come to mind about marriage when you consider the illustration of a pair of scissors. God has joined sinners in marriage. Imperfections should not shock the partners, but rather they should be ready to apply love and forgiveness. God has joined saints, when both are believers in Christ, and this calls for mutual respect. God has joined lovers, and this leads to a life on the highest level (Eph. 5:21-25). God has joined sexes. Sex relations are reserved for the intimacies of marriage. In marriage God removes the fence from between the sexes and places the fence around the sexes. This is God's design for happiness (1 Cor. 7:1-7; 1 Peter 3:1-7; Heb. 13:4). God has joined helpers in marriage (Gen. 2:18). Helping each other walk the way to heaven is the fulfillment of marriage and the home.

Jesus visited a marriage at Cana and thereby blessed all marriages in His name (John 2:1-11). He helped in the small matter of providing refreshments for the guests, and He is surely able and willing to help in the bigger matters. He can change the quality of married life as surely as He turned the water into the best wine if His presence is invited.

God directed Abraham to seek out a partner for his

son Isaac. He was a bearer of God's covenant promise. This involved faith in the true God. You can read about this in Genesis 24. Believing Rebecca became the wife of Isaac.

HOW TO BE HAPPY

Materials: A rose with stem fairly well leafed. A rose with stem and thorns exposed. A bud vase for displaying.

In many ways life is like the thorny stem of a rose with a beautiful, fragrant flower on top. (Display thorn-exposed rose in bud vase.)

How about at school? You work hard. You get some things wrong. You accept correction. You do better. In the end you have a good report, and, best of all, you are blessed with a growing mind. The thorns and rose go together.

At home you sometimes disobey. You don't act your age. You are disciplined so that you do right for a happier, better life. Thorns and the rose again.

And at church you learn lessons from the Bible. In them you are told about your faults and sins. That hurts. It punctures your pride. You feel sorrow because you failed God. The lessons also point you to God's forgiving love in Jesus. You experience the joy of being forgiven and your faith grows. More and more you want Jesus to rule your heart. So you find His kind of happiness. That's the rose on the end of the thorny stem. (Law and Gospel)

But if you just concentrated on the thorns — the hard work and corrections at school, the disciplining at home, the seeing of your sins in God's law — then you'd be hurt and have no joy. (Pinch the stem with thorns exposed.) Oh, that hurts! Do you know what some people enjoy doing? They look around for problems and troubles. They love to talk to others about their troubles. They are gloomy and pessimistic about life in general. They always see the bad side of things. They are the ones who see a half glass of water half empty instead of half full. So they worry about problems. Life is a bundle of hurts. That's like cutting off the rose and displaying the stem for the sake of the thorns. (Demonstrate it.)

Yet God has made roses to grow on thorny stems for some reason. You learn to accept that fact. If you want the beauty and fragrance of roses, you must put up with the thorns. God has made the stem manageable too. He has created roses with plenty of leaves on the stem. If you don't squeeze it too hard, you don't even feel the thorns. (Mount the rose with leafed stem.) Jesus tells us, as He told His disciples in the Upper Room, that we can expect tribulation in this world where not everyone loves Him. We can expect the natural problems that go with living, like pain, sorrow, and problems of growing old. But in all of life's thorns, we are to look to the top of the stem and see the beautiful rose. God has made our lives beautiful, and we can manage through life's trials because of Jesus, His Son. In a love story of the Old Testament He is called the Rose of Sharon (Song of Sol. 2:1). He excels in the beauty of saving love. He earned forgiveness for us. He assures us that trials and troubles are never punishments. They are sanctified in Him. The most beautiful flower of faith blooms on the top of the thorny stem.

Jesus once instructed His disciples that they should not get "hung up" on the cares of this life or worry about tomorrow's troubles (Matt. 6:24-34). In other words, Jesus says, "Don't look for thorns," "Carry the stem softly," "Enjoy the rose." Read His recipe for happiness shared with the crowd (Matt. 5:1-12). He instructed His disciples in the Upper Room about how to be happy (John

16:20-24). Paul had that joy even in prison (Phil. 4:4-7). Christians at Thessalonica were likewise joyful. (2 Thess. 1:3-4)

Why not read about this in the Book of Ruth. In the midst of the thorny history, as recorded in the Book of Judges, there is the rose of Ruth's life. Thorns in her life, yes! She knew where to look to find happiness. Naomi displayed her hurts. Thorns were mounted in her vase of life as she said to her old friends at Bethlehem: "Do not call me Naomi, call me Mara, for the Almighty has dealt very bitterly with me. I went away full, and the Lord has brought me back empty. Why call me Naomi, when the Lord has afflicted me and the Almighty has brought this calamity upon me?" (Ruth 1:20-21). Consider Ruth's attitude in contrast.

When you feel like squeezing the stem of life, stop and think about Jesus. Let the song of faith fill your heart about Him, your beautiful Savior. He wants your life to bloom like a rose. He wants its beauty and fragrance to sweeten the lives of others. He helps us through the thorniest problem of all when He leads us through the valley of the shadow of death to the joys of His house in heaven. There we shall bloom like a rose in the perfection of glory. (Psalm 23)

IMITATING JESUS

Materials: Four books: an encyclopedia volume, a health book, a Bible, and a book on social studies. Four boys will hold the books.

Who in the group is an "A" student, or nearest to being an "A" student? Come here and hold this volume of an encyclopedia as a symbol of your wisdom. Who is tallest? That is quite obvious. Come and hold a health book as a symbol of your health. Who has a good church and Sunday school attendance record? Come and hold the Bible. It is the Word of God for everyone. Who has deep concern for other people? Come and hold this book on social studies as a symbol of your social concern.

I want you to observe that not every boy excels in all four virtues in the same degree. It is commendable and praiseworthy for Christians to excel in what gifts they receive from God. Yet virtues vary. Do you think that anyone could excel in these four virtues perfectly? "Well," you say, "I don't think so." You are right. There is not a perfect student, or a perfectly healthy person, or anyone who has perfect love for God's Word, or anyone who has perfect concern for others. The reason for it is that we are all hampered by a sinful nature. And so we should realize that all our efforts to live perfect lives and be saved by our own efforts are vain.

I want to introduce One to you who has a perfect record in these four virtues — and in everything else in His life. It says of the boy Jesus at age twelve: "And Jesus increased in wisdom and in stature and in favor with God and man" (Luke 2:52). He could do this because He was perfect, without sin. (Luke 1:35; 1 Peter 2:22)

Jesus is very special or unique. He has the very nature of God in a real human nature. The mystery of His becoming flesh is that He stopped the full use of the powers of His divine nature so He could be born a baby, grow up to manhood, and go the way of the cross to die for the sins of the world. He let all the disfavor of God against the sinful world fall on His holy person as God-man, so that the world could be favored with God's forgiveness. So what we see about the boy Jesus at twelve is a glimpse of that perfect life which He later offered on the cross as a sin-offering in His manhood.

Do you boys trust Jesus as your Savior? Your answer is yes. That makes you sons of God. Jesus is your Big Brother. As you trust Him to save you, you are given new desires to imitate Jesus. You have the joy of imitating Jesus by "growing in wisdom and in stature and in favor with God and man."

Jesus "increased in wisdom." Jesus humbled Himself. He didn't fully use His all-knowledge as God, so He grew in knowledge from the human side. Yet always with the divine purpose, "In whom are hid all the treasures of wisdom and knowledge" (Col. 2:3). Do you do the very best you can at school and at all opportunities of Christian learning and service? Jesus would want you to be the best possible servant of God. He wants you to contribute the highest values possible to His kingdom and to society. Your life and work is like a pulpit from which you proclaim the Christian values of life.

Jesus "increased in stature." He grew physically. He knew it was important to eat the right foods to build up His body. You know He stayed away from body-destroying abuses (name some). His body had no defects. Ours do. So we have to get medical and dental checkups, eye examinations, and the like. He would want us to take care of the body we have, in which is housed a saved soul.

Jesus "increased in favor with God." He grew spiritually; that is, from the human side He grew in spiritual experience with God's love and favor. (Have child with Bible read Is. 11:2.) Later His Father testified of that favor (Matt. 3:17; 17:5). God our Father testifies of this to us (Gal. 4:4-7). We are sons of God. Our joyful task in life is to live out before others what we are in God's sight. Think what favor with God means when tempted to do wrong, when you seem to stand alone for what's honest and true! You with God make a majority in any situation. So grow up in that favor. Know that God is always forgiving you as you keep living by faith in Jesus. Experience how good it is to feel accepted, loved, and secure. Grow up in that love which passes all knowledge.

Jesus "increased in favor with man." He grew socially. Jesus loved people. He "went about doing good." He was courteous and kind. This drew people to Him. Followers of Jesus will by their good deeds leave their mark on the social order of which they are a part. Loving the neighbor as they love themselves attracts people to God. It might be fashionable to be "rough and tough" and to imitate the ways of evil, but love and goodness always win out. (1 Peter 2:12; John 13:34-35)

We sing in a hymn:

> I lay my sins on Jesus,
> The spotless Lamb of God;
> He bears them all and frees us
> From the accursed load.

And we continue by singing:

I long to be like Jesus,
Meek, loving, lowly, mild;
I long to be like Jesus,
The Father's holy Child.
(*The Lutheran Hymnal,* 652)

Think about that. You *are* the Father's holy child in Jesus.
Read Ephesians 4; Heb. 5:5 — 6:12; 1 Thessalonians 1;
2 Tim. 1:1-14; 1 Kings 3, Solomon's wisdom; Eph. 6:4;
1 Peter 2:21-25.

LIFE'S LITTLE THINGS

Materials: A stickpin and pin cushion; a box with a few paper clips; a container of small nails. Have a few sheets of paper handy, sheets that belong together, to demonstrate the use of paper clips.

(Show the stickpin.) This is just a little item. Perhaps you cannot even see it from where you are. It's a stickpin. Can you name some important uses for stickpins? Patterns are held to the cloth with stickpins. Hems are set with them. Name tags are attached to a person's clothing with them too. They are little but useful, aren't they?

(Show a paper clip.) What is this item used for? I mean, its proper use. Often a paper clip is straightened out to make a piece of wire to repair things. This is not the proper use for a paper clip. Rather, its main use is to hold papers together that belong together. Here are some papers on the same subject that should not be separated and lost. Individual sheets would be useless. Perhaps a staple could do the job. Yet there are times when a paper clip is better, especially when the sheets must be spread out later for side-by-side viewing.

(Show a nail.) In your home there are many of these items. They are out of sight, but are doing the great work of holding the structure together. (Perhaps the building you are in is built with nails. In that event make that your illustration, and contrast the importance of little nails compared with a piano or organ in the classroom or church. The little things, out of sight, are really important.)

Do you agree that life's little things are very important? Let's apply this idea to spiritual matters. The Bible has much to say on this. A little word means much. "A word in season, how good it is!" (Prov. 15:23). A little deed. Andrew did many little things compared with his brother Simon Peter (John 1:40-42; 6:8; 20:22). A little person said a rather unimportant thing, but it led to great blessings. The maid from the land of Israel said the right words, which led to Naaman's healing (2 Kings 5). Esther was but one little person in a strange land. She did what she could to hold things together for her people. Her uncle Mordecai reminded her: "If you keep silence at such a time as this, relief and deliverance will rise for the Jews from another quarter, but you and your father's house will perish. And who knows whether you have not come to the kingdom for such a time as this?" (Esther 4:14). That race was kept together by "one paper clip" so that a Savior could come into the world through that race. The shepherd boy David became king of Israel to build a mighty nation for that purpose. (1 Sam. 16:10-13)

When we do our humble duties, life's little things, it all adds up to much. Let's not forget the smile that brightens the day for others, the word of encouragement that keeps others going the right way, and the word of witness about Jesus the Savior which leads them on the saving way. So this is what our life is all about. It is to hold things together in this temporal life for the eternal kingdom of Christ. Life has a divine pattern in Christ, and like the pins and the pattern, we are to bear witness to that. The weak in faith need to be encouraged by the Word to stay with Christ and in fellowship with other Christians. Like a paper clip with papers, we do what we can. The kingdom of Christ must be built by proclaiming His Word at home and abroad, so like the little nails, we do what building we can.

For the pin to do its part and not become a reject, it must be kept shiny and sharp. It must not get weathered by being left outside. Stickpins are kept in a pin cushion inside the house for handy use. As Christians we must be in places only that befit a Christian (Psalm 1). Paper clips are usually kept in a box in a desk drawer. Nails are kept inside, out of the weather, to keep them shiny. Nails must be kept in containers. Otherwise they will be scattered around, and you know how they can even get into a bicycle or car tire. A Christian can do harm to others and harm the kingdom of Christ by being in the wrong places. Lessons taught by bad example are hard to erase. Life is made up of a lot of little things. It's the little things that Jesus takes into account, too. (Matt. 25:34-40)

The way to keep doing humble things is to be a humble person. John the Baptizer said: "He must increase, but I must decrease" (John 3:30). That is the secret. We can afford to be humble people when we remember that what we are and have is all because of God's love to us in Jesus Christ. Peter advised young Christians: "Clothe your-selves, all of you, with humility toward one another" (1 Peter 5:5). (Rom. 12:16 TEV reminds us to accept humble duties.)

As a child you may seem small in a world of adults with big programs. But you are very important. Jesus said so (Mark 10:13-16). You are even an example of faith to adults. Keep doing life's little things.

NO DEPOSIT — NO RETURN

Materials: A "no deposit — no return" soft-drink bottle. A returnable milk bottle.

(Display the soft-drink bottle. Have pupils read the "No Deposit — No Return" marking.) Do you know that some people's lives are like that? You ask, "How so?" The plain answer is that they do not accept the payment the Lord Jesus made. They consider their lives a cheap thing. They think they are here to live just for themselves because at the end of life they will end up on the human "trash heap" anyway. They refuse to believe that they are redeemed for the abundant life now and the life eternal that is to come. The Bible says: "You know that you were ransomed from the futile ways inherited from your fathers, not with perishable things such as silver or gold, but with the precious blood of Christ, like that of a lamb without blemish or spot" (1 Peter 1:18-19). It also says: "You are not your own; you were bought with a price. So glorify God in your body." (1 Cor. 6:19-20)

When people refuse to believe that they are redeemed by the precious blood of Christ, they usually find an escape in a selfish life of pleasure seeking. The bottle we use here merely as a symbol of the pleasure life. The apostle Paul mentioned the pleasure type in Phil. 3:19: "Their end is destruction, their god is the belly, and they glory in their shame, with minds set on earthly things." Some Bible examples of the selfish life are these: the Herod family (Mark 6:17-24); Nebuchadnezzar (Daniel 5); Judas (Matt.

27:3-5; Acts 1:15-20); the servants in the parable. (Matt. 25:24-30)

The final outcome of such living apart from faith in Christ is evident. It is not an end of existence by some imagined disintegration on a trash heap. It is rather abiding under God's wrath (John 3:36b). More is said in Matt. 25:41-46; 2 Tim. 3:1-9; 2 Thess. 1:7-10; and the Epistle of Jude.

(Display the milk bottle.) Here is an ordinary milk bottle. This bottle will represent the true Christian who lives by faith in Jesus Christ. This bottle does not belong to itself but to the dairy that has bought it for the purpose of distributing milk. Thus the Bible reminds us in connection with being bought with a price that "you are not your own." When buying milk in a bottle of this type, you make a deposit, don't you? That deposit is to remind you that the bottle is not yours, but that it belongs to the dairy and that it is to be returned to the dairy. So true Christians realize that they are not their own making, but that they are created in Christ Jesus for good works by God's grace (Eph. 2:8-10). Since Christ has bought us, He has a right to what is His. As we are careful not to break the milk bottles for which a deposit is made, so we are careful to live our lives in His service. We do that as we remember the great price Christ paid to redeem us and make us what we are— His workmanship!

Milk bottles are for being filled with milk. They do not fulfill their purpose if they are left standing in the garage or porch to collect dust. They do not fulfill their purpose if used for watering plants. As Christians we have one main purpose in life—to share the Gospel with others. We are to be filled with the "milk" of God's Word (1 Peter 2:2). This makes us "containers" for the distribution or sharing of that soul-saving food to others. If we live for a lesser purpose, we fail our main purpose. If we refuse to share the Gospel, we are like dusty bottles in a dark place somewhere.

Only as we remember that Christ paid the all-sufficient price will we let faith abound in thanksgiving and joyful sharing. There is a "return" on the life of service now. It is the daily dividend of joy to us who serve. And to Christ it is the daily thanksgiving. Someone has said that what you are as a Christian is Christ's gift to you, and what you do as a Christian is your gift to Him. There will also be a "return" of eternal reward (Matt. 25:16-23; 34-40; 46b; compare 2 Tim. 4:6-8; 1 Cor. 3:14; Dan. 12:3). Read about the apostle Paul's spiritual attitude as one who lived in the constant knowledge of the price Christ paid for him (1 Tim. 6:6-19; 1 Cor. 15:9-11). What are you doing with your life? Remember, "no deposit — no return."

NOT ASHAMED OF THE GOSPEL

Materials: Luther's Christian coat of arms made vari-dimensional. The black cross should be made of wood. A bolt should be inserted through the cross, which is long enough to hold the red heart, the white five-petaled rose, and the field of blue and gold. These items can be made of thick corrugated cardboard.

(Display cross.) Do you know that some people don't know the meaning of the cross? I wish to tell you about one person especially who didn't know what it meant for him. His name was Martin Luther. He was brought up on teachings which were often different from the Bible. He was told that the way to get right with God was to do good works, fast, and pray. When his conscience found no peace, he tried harder, even taking up monastic life in order to have more time to pray. He increased his prayer formula to twenty-one saints a week—three a day. His body became weak with fastings and hard work. But he found no peace.

At the same time he studied and taught in universities. In 1512 he became a doctor of divinity. This meant he could study the whole Bible and lecture from it. As he read the Bible, especially the Psalms, Romans, and Galatians, he found what the cross meant. When studying Rom. 1:16-17 he said, "I've found it, I've found it." He read: "I am not ashamed of the Gospel: it is the power of God for salvation to everyone who has faith . . . . He who through faith is righteous shall live." He realized that God made His Son Jesus Christ to be sin for the whole world. So Luther believed that he and every sinner can lay his sins on Jesus and experience the power of God in personal salvation by faith alone.

(Place red heart behind the cross.) When Luther found peace with God through faith in the Christ of the cross, he found that his heart lived by faith covered with the blood of Christ (Rom. 10:9-10). Besides, a heart covered with the blood of Christ is a courageous heart. Luther dared to speak out and confess this saving truth of the Gospel. He brought it out from behind monastic walls to the arena of everyday life. He wrote ninety-five sentences to point out the many false teachings and to point to what was right. In one of them he said: "The true treasure of the church is the holy Gospel of the glory and of the grace of God." (Thesis 62)

Are you a courageous believer? To believe that Jesus lived and died long ago might amount to mere history unless you believe: "He lived and died for me." When you firmly believe that, there is no holding back in sharing it with others, is there?

(Place the rose behind the cross and heart.) What is symbolized by the white rose? It is a symbol of the fact that when you believe in your heart that Jesus died for your sins, you are declared one hundred percent perfect in God's sight because of Jesus' holiness. In fact the rose represents Christ, who is called in prophecy the Rose of Sharon. (Song of Sol. 2:1)

Notice that the rose has five petals. We will let each petal represent a spiritual area of our lives. In doing this let us note how things were in Luther's early life and time and how they should be in our daily life.

Petal one — WORSHIP. Think how Luther's "worship" life in his early years was mainly form and routine (2 Tim. 3:5). True worship is a loving and living response to Christ's love. It flows from a heart renewed by living faith. St. Paul explains worship in these words: "Present your bodies as a living sacrifice, holy and acceptable to God, which is your spiritual worship." (Rom. 12:1)

Petal two — EDUCATION. In Luther's day the Bible was a closed book to the common people. Luther translated it into the common language of the people. Education of course is not just learning Bible facts. It is grasping Christ (see the cross in the center) and believing in Him (the red heart). We have the blessing of the Bible in our language. Let us therefore study it and grow in grace mightily. (2 Peter 3:18)

Petal three — STEWARDSHIP. In Luther's day the cross was a hidden power. So stewardship was reduced to fund raising, often of the worst kind. The church even sold indulgences (they were said to shorten the suffering of poor souls in purgatory — a mere human invention). When the church loses its Gospel power, there is no end of schemes for raising funds. True stewardship expresses the practical way of Christian living in which everything is placed under Christ's management: self, service, and substance. First men are raised to new life, then self is consecrated to His service, and firstfruit giving of material blessings follows from the heart.

Petal four — PRAYER. A lot of words, to saints and even to Mary! Is that prayer? Luther found it was not. Rather, true prayer is faith that talks with God from the heart (Is. 63:16; Ps. 19:14). It is always in Jesus' name, that is, in the framework of His redeeming love (John 16:23). Keep in mind the cross on the heart, as in this illustration, when you think of prayer. Prayer is the result of being a believer, not the way to become one. When we become believers, we do what is becoming to a believer, and that is to talk with our heavenly Father about getting His will done more and more in our daily living. (Rom. 8:26-27; 1 John 5:14)

Petal five — EVANGELISM. Perhaps Luther never heard of it before the Reformation. The church was like a refrigerator, keeping partial truth and man-made religious recipes on ice! But with the personal discovery of the cross, Luther found his heart aflame, willing to share with the world what it means to have Christ's perfection as declared in the Gospel. He preached, taught, and wrote to friend and foe in a continuing effort to confess the Gospel of Christ. Are you sharing the Gospel?

In all these areas we act out of love to Christ. We grow in the expression of these just as a rose grows. The rose also stands for Christian joy. It is a joy to serve Jesus Christ.

(Attach cross, heart, and rose to blue and gold background.) Our joy is not marred by the fact that someday we must leave this world. Blue stands for our heavenly hope, the blue of heaven where Jesus ascended to prepare a place for us. "We rejoice in our hope of sharing the glory of God" (Rom. 5:2). There is no purgatory of suffering to mar our hope. Heaven is ours by faith in Christ. The hope of heaven is surrounded by a circle of gold. Heaven is precious to us. It is the security of the golden city, the heavenly Jerusalem. Forever we shall be with the Lord. (Rev. 21:2, 18)

NOT GOOD IF DETACHED

Materials: A round box a few inches deep. The lid
should be brown on the outside and gray on the inside.
Outline a heart in brown on the inside, the full size of the
lid. The base should be green, with the bottom gold on
the outside. For within the base prepare a white heart
the size of the one on the lid, with a red cross on it the
full length of the heart. Attach a green ribbon about 18"
long from the tip of the heart to the bottom of the base.
Attach some stewardship items to the ribbon: a small
calendar for *TIME*, a pencil for *TALENT,* and a dollar
bill for *TREASURE.* The lid will be attached to the cross
and heart, so prepare some device to attach it. (A safety
pin will work.)

(Display the lid.) Here is an item that might have some
use in life. What is this item? Perhaps you are thinking that
it is a tray or something. If it were not made of paper,
perhaps it could be used for an ash tray. Upon closer exam-
ination it appears that it is a lid that belongs to a box.
(Show the base and demonstrate how the lid fits on the
base.)

I have spiritualized these items to illustrate a basic
lesson for life. The lid is brown and stands for our mortal
nature, "dust to dust, ashes to ashes." Jesus said: "That
which is born of flesh is flesh" (John 3:6). But the problem
goes deeper. It is an internal one. The inside of this lid is
gray. On the gray is an outline of a heart. The gray represents the darkness of eternal death. Every human heart is

under that judgment by nature because of sin (Rom. 6:23a). The circle reminds us that eternal death is to exist apart from God forever.

The base of the box is green in color and round in shape to represent eternal life. Inside the box are items that remind us of Christ's gracious salvation. (Show just the heart and cross and let them go back into the base.) This base and its contents will stand for Christ's kingdom of grace with its offer of eternal life. Just as this base is made to fit the lid, so Christ's salvation is prepared by God to meet our spiritual need. This salvation is offered during the period of one's lifetime, which is every sinner's personal time of grace. The time of grace is opportunity to become attached to Christ. (Show how the gray heart can be attached to the cross and white heart.) Like the lid and base belong together, so sinners and Christ belong together.

God acted in love and sent His Son to redeem lost mankind. His Son suffered and died on the cross and shed His precious blood for that redemption. The Holy Spirit works through that Gospel message to attach sinners to Christ by bringing them to faith. The lid did not join the cross by any power in itself; sinners cannot come to Christ except by the power of the Holy Spirit (1 Cor. 12:3). When sinners become attached to Christ by faith, this results in personal forgiveness and newness of life, as illustrated by this white heart. God accepts you and me in Christ. There is also the gift of spiritual and eternal life. (Show how the ribbon is attached to the heart and anchored to the base.) (You will find a fuller explanation of the loving action of the Triune God in this redemption in Eph. 1:3-14.)

When God gives new hearts through Christ, He gives new motives to live a new life. Christ is in control of that life just as the cross is in the center of the heart. The gifts of life are seen in new perspective and are used under the management of the new heart. The gifts of life are used in line with eternal life just as this green ribbon is attached to the base. Perhaps you noticed some items attached to the ribbon, and you are wondering what they mean.

The first item is a calendar. It reminds us that time is a gift of God. Time is opportunity to come into possession of our most needed gift: new birth by faith in Christ. No one knows how much time he has to prepare for eternity. So the Bible urgently insists that now is the accepted time (2 Cor. 6:2). Time is opportunity for service. Jesus made it thus (John 9:14). The next item is a pencil. This stands for talents. By talents I don't mean only special aptitudes, but the basic talents that everyone has for serving God and others in this life through one's occupation. A pencil reminds you that already as children at school you are using your talents that God has given you (Rom. 12:6-8; Matt. 25:14-46). The third item is a dollar bill. Money is a gift of God too. It is time and talent applied. Money must be under the new management or else it becomes an idol (1 Tim. 6:10-11, 17-19). Our bodies and minds are gifts of God too (1 Cor. 6:19-20; Phil. 4:8). These and whatever else God gives must be used in line with our eternal calling. So we live in view of heaven. We use our lives to witness the Gospel of Christ—by living and sharing, with words, deeds, and gifts. A big word for life under new management during this time of grace is stewardship. It means to manage our life with all its gifts from God for the good of Christ's kingdom. "As each has received a gift, employ it for one another, as good stewards of God's varied grace" (1 Peter 4:10). His grace makes it possible for us to be newborn sons of eternal life. We dedicate ourselves to living as His sons to lead others to life.

So as this sinful heart is attached to the cross for newness of life and purpose, so we live in Christ in line with eternal life. If the lid with the sinful heart is detached, it falls under judgment. It is God's sustaining grace, and only that, which makes the difference between eternal life and eternal separation from God. The offer is made in the time of grace. As the lid finds purpose in being a cover for the base, so lost sinners find purpose only in relationship to Christ and His grace, and the gift is eternal life (Rom. 6:23). At the moment of death each person is considered "in Christ" or "apart from Christ." If there is no attachment to Christ, there is eternal separation (Matt. 25:24-30). (You might demonstrate this point by detaching the lid. Point out again that as a circle it represents the eternal separation from Christ and God.) But by faith in Christ there is life; and besides, there is the faithful stewardship life to evidence the reality of faith (Matt. 25:16-23). (Reattach lid.)

There are some things this box cannot show us, as the fact that in the heaven of eternal life we will no longer have a sinful nature. We will be renewed in the perfect image of God (Ps. 17:15). Perhaps this box can give us a glimpse of this glory as we turn it sideways and see the bottom. It is a circle of gold to represent eternal glory. From this point of view the old sinful nature is hidden from view. From the point of view of glory the nature of sin will be a thing of the past, hidden in the grave. Let us remember that it is of vital importance to be attached to Christ. With that attachment the faithful stewardship life will follow and evidence true faith.

THE POWER OF CHRISTIAN EXAMPLE

Materials: Two cans of fruit, two boxes of cereal, and two packages of potato chips. One of each of the items should be displayed without the impressive advertising. Take the paper label off the fruit, and mark the can with the name of the fruit within. Put a plain brown paper around the cereal box, and mark it with the cereal within. For the potato chips use a plain brown sack into which you have stuffed some paper as filler, and mark it "Potato Chips." Display the items together. You might "mess up" the plain items somewhat with scribblings. You will need a shopping bag. (In this lesson we are using peaches and Wheaties.)

(Invite two children to come forward. One will do the shopping, the other will observe.)

Sometimes mother needs certain items from the store. She asks, "Who will run the errand?" Which one wants to do the shopping today? (Give bag to the shopper.) Suppose mother wants a can of peaches, a box of Wheaties, and a package of potato chips. So you go to the grocery store, and this is what you see. (Naturally the child will take the items with the impressive advertising.) (Ask the observer if he would have made the same choices.) Now children, why did you choose the items which you did? Because they looked nicer, is a pretty good answer. Can you see any connection with this and Christian life? Have you realized that lives that spell honesty, kindness, truth are impressive advertisements for Christ? Would people be led to consider the claims of Christ if your and my life were wrapped up in the desires of the flesh, like these messed-up wrappings?

This box of Wheaties is just as genuine as the other. (Show it with wrappings off.) Yet how could the shopper know it unless it was revealed on the outside? Besides, if advertising people know how important it is to make a Wheaties box so impressive, we Christians ought to know how important it is to dress up our lives in Christian attitudes. Suppose you call each other names when you play in your neighborhood, or argue, what are people led to think? Or maybe you have to be scolded a lot because you don't like obeying, so right at home you give a bad example. Or could it be that you find it hard to forgive when others hurt or insult you? At such times you are like these messed-up items, aren't you?

Impressive advertising tells clearly what is in the containers. You don't have to go so far as to shake the can of peaches or press the Wheaties box and the potato chips to find out. That's not a very good way to shop. So a person may say, "I am a Christian because I believe in Christ." That is, of course, true. The product of true faith is in the heart. But true faith must show itself on the outside in the fruits of the Spirit. (Gal. 5:22-25)

We are in the world to relate the Gospel of Christ to others. Jesus made that clear in Matt. 5:14-16. The apostle Paul explained to Christians at Corinth the power of Christian example. In 2 Cor. 3:1-5 he reminded them that their faith and Christian living were sufficient advertising for the truth and power of Christ's Gospel. Paul said that he didn't need letters from anyone for the genuineness of his ministry. The fruit of the Gospel in their lives was proof enough. Their lives stood out like public monuments in the city square. But this difference: their engraving was by the

Spirit of God, not on markers of stone but on tablets of the human heart. (We might say, Christians are Christ's "P. R." people, "P. R." for public relations.) When faith shows itself in true fruits of the Spirit, there is real public relations going on. People are directed to our Redeemer when they see that we are really redeemed. Paul said: "You yourselves are our letter of recommendation written on your hearts, to be known and read by all men, and you show that you are a letter from Christ delivered by us" (2 Cor. 3:2-3). These people could advertise for Christ because the Gospel of Christ did wonders for them. (1 Cor. 6:9-11)

It is that way with us too. Christ gives us faith for inner cleansing. The faith He gives is Spirit-worked life and power. It goes into action for Spirit-powered living. Christ then makes a real, noticeable difference in daily life. The chief purpose of the Gospel is to bring people to saving knowledge of Christ. Its good news brings deliverance from the penalty and guilt of sin. This is called "justification by faith." A person can stand right with God by faith in Christ. Connected with this truth is "sanctification from or in faith." Saved people take a stand against sin and imitate Christ's holiness. Jesus said that these two truths belong together. (Matt. 7:15-20)

Think of the power of Christian example. If you are a child, youth, or adult; if you are at home, at work, or at play, you are always advertising, either for or against Christ. If you are never seen reading your Bible or folding your hands in prayer; or never heard speaking a word about Christ and His church (except perhaps to criticize); or if you use profane words, slander, dirty talk, and cheat besides, then you are like messed-up containers. People pass them by. And the tragedy is, there are no others to choose from. The only ones given the task of advertising for Christ are the Christians. So what if we fail?

The power of Christian example is expressed in the lives of early Christians: 1 Peter 3:8 to 4:19; Stephen, Acts 6:8-15; Josiah, 2 Kings 22; Simeon and Anna, Luke 2:25-38; and the message of 3 John. A contrast is found in Acts 5:1-11, the case of Ananias and Sapphira.

REFLECTING THE LORD'S GLORY

Materials: A mirror a foot high or more; an electric light bulb on an extension cord; a picture of Jesus framed in gold; a black cloth to be used as a veil. Your face and some children's faces will be used in the demonstration.

Here is a handy object. (Display the mirror.) What use is a mirror? Its purpose is to produce a reflection of the object or objects near it. You look into it to see if your hair is combed properly and in general to check your appearance. (Display light bulb and plug it in.) Here is another handy object. Electric lights bring so much brightness into our daily life. We will let this light stand for our Lord Jesus, who is the Light of the world. He brightens up our lives in a spiritual way with His saving glory. To make sure we do not forget what this light stands for, I will attach a picture of Jesus behind the light. Now as I hold these before the mirror, the light and picture with the gold is reflected like a "blaze of glory."

As I hold the picture and the light before the mirror, I am in the background. My face is rather dark way back there in the shadows. Would any of you students like to look and see how you look in the background darkness? How is it possible to shine with the light of Jesus? That's pretty simple when you think about it. Simply come closer to the light that is reflected in the mirror. When you move your face into "the Jesus light" you find His very glory shining on your face. Who would like to look? (If there is time and the class is not too large, have everyone look.) Now you know how to have a beautiful face that shines with the Lord's glory.

This demonstration, in a way, illustrates what the apostle Paul said in 2 Cor. 3:18: "All of us, then, reflect the glory of the Lord with uncovered faces; and that same glory, coming from the Lord who is the Spirit, transforms us into His very likeness, in an ever greater degree of glory" (TEV). Remember how dark our faces were as we stood in the background; then how the reflection of our Lord's glory increased on our faces as we came closer to the light? Well, that is what the apostle is talking about. He found the saving light of Jesus. It all started for him in the Damascus road experience when the bright light from heaven flashed about him. The voice from that light was that of the Lord Jesus. Paul saw His saving glory with eyes of faith (Acts 9:1-19). He made quite a point of his Lord's saving glory when he wrote to Christians at Corinth the second time. He said that to see and reflect the Lord's glory is the joyous privilege of every person. (2 Cor. 3:7-18)

If a person persists in refusing to believe in Jesus as Lord, then it is like putting a veil over the head so the glory of the Lord cannot be seen. Many of the people of Israel were like that in Paul's time. (Who would like to demonstrate this point by placing the veil over your head?) There is no light reflected on your face as you wear the veil. So the apostle made an emphatic point of being in the Lord's light with unveiled faces. First there is the light that comes by believing in Jesus as personal Savior. Then there is the light of faith that is reflected in our way of life because we let Jesus make a real difference. It is like light on our faces when we stand in the light. The closer we live to Jesus' light, the greater will be the reflection, and the more we will be transformed into His very likeness.

It is important to know what Jesus is like before we will be interested in being transformed into His likeness. Jesus is truthful. He said to Pilate: "Everyone who is of the truth hears My voice" (John 18:37). Do you aim to be like Jesus in truthfulness from the heart? Some people live by the "eleventh commandment," which says, "Break all the other ten, just don't get caught." They cheat if it is convenient and lie if it is to their immediate advantage. What do you do? Jesus is kind and forgiving. He forgave those who crucified Him (Luke 23:34). Do you try to apply forgiveness? Some say they forgive and will bury the ax, but they leave the handle sticking out so they can use it at the slightest irritation. Real forgiveness is to forgive from the heart and treat the other person as if he had never offended you (Eph. 4:32). Think of other ways you can imitate Jesus. (See Gal. 5:22-23)

Remember that staying close to the light means, in a spiritual way, that you avail yourself of His light in His Word. Read it, Hear it. Listen to it. Live it. Obey it. Eph. 5:1-4 gives us a contrast between the way of darkness, unbelief, and immorality, and living the new life in the light. John the Baptizer lived in the Lord's light and reflected His glory (John 1:4-9, 15, 19-37; Luke 1:76-80; 3:1-20). Compare Luke 2:8-14 and John 8:12 with Luke 2:25-32 and Matt. 5:14-16 concerning the Lord's glory and our reflecting it.

The gold frame around the picture of Jesus can remind us of the glory of heaven. Jesus is our Lord, the heavenly King. We shall share in that glory as we receive Him now as Savior and Lord. Will you let His glory be seen upon you? (Rev. 21:10, 18, 22-27)

> Renew me, O eternal Light,
> And let my heart and soul be bright,
> Illumined with the light of grace
> That issues from Thy holy face.
> (*The Lutheran Hymnal*, 398)

SALT-OF-THE-EARTH CHRISTIANS

Materials: A number of saltshakers: one plain, one ornate, one small, and one large. One should have salt in it.

(Shake some salt on your hand. Put a few grains on your tongue. Let pupils do the same.) Salt is such a simple thing. Yet it is such a great gift of the Creator. Food would be flat and tasteless without salt.

Jesus said about Christians: "You are the salt of the earth" (Matt. 5:13). We must remember that men do not make salt, just gather it. Likewise Christians are not self-made, but Christ-made. He gives new life. "We are His workmanship, created in Christ Jesus for good works, which God prepared beforehand, that we should walk in them" (Eph. 2:10). Ps. 100:3 says: "Know that the Lord is God! It is He that made us, and we are His; we are His people." To be a Christian is a great gift!

Let us think of ways we all can be salt-of-the-earth Christians.

When you put some salt on your tongue, your taste buds are really stimulated, aren't they? This can remind us of one way we can be salt-of-the-earth Christians. It says in Col. 4:6: "Let your speech always be gracious, seasoned with salt, so that you may know how you ought to answer everyone." Speech seasoned with salt doesn't mean making small talk, nor does it involve saying "sweet nothings" to make up polite conversation. Salty speech has good taste. It shows respect. It may delight, astonish, even irritate the hearer. When your parents speak words of correction, it may irritate, but it's for your good. Salty speech makes people thirsty for Christ, just like salt on popcorn makes us thirsty for water. Jesus said what needed to be said to the woman at the well, and she thirsted for the Water of life (John 4). Daniel used salty speech in a difficult situation (Daniel 1). The apostle Paul used salty speech in his witnessing (Acts 13:13-43; 17:16-34). Peter instructed Christians in the right type of speech. (1 Peter 3:13-16)

Another way we can be salt-of-the-earth Christians is by living upright lives. What use has salt besides for seasoning food? In days of old before the invention of deep freezers and refrigerators, food that was to be kept a long time had to be preserved with salt, especially meats. The process is still used today. When Jesus said that Christians are the salt of the earth, he meant that society would rot with evil and go to ruin except for the preserving quality which Christians add by upright living. Where Christians are, there is truth, honesty, love, goodwill, and other fruits of the Spirit (Gal. 5:22). This is because the Holy Spirit is working within us to make faith active in doing good (1 Cor. 6:9-11). The apostle Paul urged the young pastor Timothy as a leader to aim at righteousness, faith, love, peace, godliness, and to set an example to others in speech, conduct, and purity (1 Tim. 4:6-13; 6:11-12; 2 Tim. 2:22). This is the calling of every Christian. Sometimes people think that the Christian calling is to revolutionize society by noisy demonstrations. Christians are even accused of being "undercover Christians" and "secret service saints." But like salt, which does its preserving work quietly, the best Christian preservative is by applying truth, honesty, love, and kindness, day by day at home, school, and the place of work. Christians are "undercover Christians" and "secret service saints" of the best kind.

Salt has still another quality. It is an antiseptic that kills germs. It can even destroy plants. Weeds that spring up between bricks on the walk or in cracks of the sidewalk can be destroyed with salt. When lawlessness and attendant evils spring up in the community, we reprove evil. In Eph. 5:3-11 the apostle Paul cataloged some of the evils that can sprout in society and said: "Take no part in the unfruitful works of darkness, but instead expose them." We can protest by nonparticipation in evil. We don't go to the immoral movie or play or read immoral literature. We can protest by bringing evils to the attention of those who are promoting them. Our action as salt will not stamp out all evil in the world, but it will make the world a more fit place in which to walk. (Psalm 1)

The seasoning, preserving, and destroying qualities of salt all depend on the amount of application. Notice that the saltshaker has a top with many tiny holes in it for sprinkling salt to season food. Did you ever have too much salt on your breakfast eggs? If you did, you will recall that it made them bitter. Salt-of-the-earth Christians ask the Lord to give them the sanctified common sense to apply the proper amount. Overcorrection may lead to anger, for example. (Eph. 6:4)

Salt must be applied to be useful. If not applied, life is not affected for good. So let us serve our Creator in Jesus Christ faithfully. It doesn't matter what our daily vocation is. (Display the plain shaker.) Some vocations are lowly in unlovely places. (Display the ornate shaker.) Some vocations are held in public esteem and get a lot of attention. Some even make people rich in material things. (Display the large shaker.) Some Christians are leaders in their church and receive much honor. They have an area of large responsibility. (Display the small shaker.) As a child you are less noticed in what you do. But every Christian has the same calling to apply the salt of preservation wherever he is. (Rom. 12:6-8; 1 Cor. 12:4-11)

SHARING THE GOOD NEWS

Materials: A Christmas card in an envelope on which is a cancelled stamp with smeared cancellation marks. (If you have a Christmas stamp with a Christian theme, like a Nativity scene, it will make possible the application of letting Christ be seen in you.)

I received a Christmas card from a friend. The card carried the message that God's Son came to earth as our Savior. His coming to our earth and His coming to our hearts by faith brings peace and joy. So this card brought me the joyful good news that I am saved by God's Son.

Now what if it had no stamp? Post offices these days make an attempt to deliver letters by delivering with a "Postage Due" note. If the receiver refuses to pay the postage, he will not get the message. So the best way to send cards and letters to friends is to stick on a stamp. Each one of us, then, is like a stamp. We give ourselves for the purpose of sharing the Good News. We are the "paid postages" by the love to Christ so that we freely share with others. Let us make some comparisons between this stamp and our Christian calling of sharing the Good News.

The stamp on the letter says, "Get the Good News Out." It's our most important task in life. Jesus said: "Go therefore and make disciples of all nations" (Matt. 28:19). He also said: "Go into all the world and preach the Gospel to the whole creation" (Mark 16:15). Like a postage stamp, we are purchased—purchased by Christ for a special task. We are not to be mounted in a cozy life of ease as a stamp in a neat collection for display. Neither are stamps placed on envelopes just for decoration. Stamps are made for sending cards and letters. Christians are for sharing the Good News. That's life's first purpose.

The stamp says, "Go where you are sent." Think of Jonah. He once refused to go. Later he went as God commanded him. Of Paul and Barnabas it is said: "Then after fasting and praying they laid their hands on them and sent them off. So, being sent out by the Holy Spirit, they went down to Seleucia; and from there they sailed to Cyprus" (Acts 13:3-4). That was just the beginning. Read on in the chapter. Do you go where sent? You are where you are as a sent one to share the Good News with your friends and neighbors. You as a young person might aspire to be a pastor, teacher, missionary. If you cannot go to other places in the world personally, are you using the extension approach—prayers and gifts? Jesus chose seventy disciples and sent them out. They went. They came back with joy. (Luke 10:1-20)

The stamp says, "Stick to your job." This stamp is stuck down firmly. If it were stuck on loosely, it might have gotten rubbed off. If the "corners" of our lives are uncommitted, then the devil, the world, and our flesh can easily use those corners to lead us to ruin like a Judas or a Demas. Again, this would hinder the progress of the card. To be "on again, off again" hinders the cause of sharing the Good News. Peter and John were told by the Jerusalem council to stop speaking the name of Jesus. But they stuck to their jobs at every turn of their lives, saying: "We cannot but speak of what we have seen and heard" (Acts 4:15-21). The apostle Paul faced difficulty at Corinth, yet he stayed on longer than usual as a traveling missionary. He stuck to his job. (Acts 18:9-11)

The stamp says, "Don't mind being smeared." Somewhere in the process of getting this card to its destination the stamp had to be canceled. That smeared the face of this stamp. Christians often get "smeared" by the godless world. Jesus said it would happen (Matt. 5:11-12). Stephen was "smeared." Some godless people instigated men who said: "We have heard him speak blasphemous words against Moses and God" (Acts 6:8-15). Paul and Barnabas got that treatment too (Acts 13:44-46). Daniel was victim of a smear campaign (Dan. 6:4-13). Early Christians to whom Peter wrote were "smeared" by their neighbors for living such good lives. They were persecuted and talked down. (1 Peter 4:12-19)

The stamp says, "Take a licking." The stamp had to be licked to make it stick. It is a truth of the Bible and an experience of Christian living that we can sometimes get harsh treatment ("take a licking") for standing up for Jesus. Paul and Silas were literally beaten with rods (Acts 16:19-25). The persecuted Christians to whom Peter wrote lost possessions and friends. Life became difficult. Yet Peter says it works for spiritual good. These people stuck to the job of living for Jesus, and they told the Good News wherever they went. They didn't find time for playing with sin (1 Peter 4:1-6). The trials and troubles of life drive us closer to Christ. Close to Him, we see His purpose and find ourselves sticking to the tasks for which we are called.

The stamp says, "Let Christ be seen in you." (This application is possible if you have a Christmas stamp with a spiritual theme.) The enemies saw Stephen's face as that of an angel (Acts 6:15). Peter and John let Jesus show (Acts 4:13). Christians of Peter's time were advised to do the same (1 Peter 3:13-18). If we let Jesus show in our living, it gives force to our telling of the Good News. Our life is a witness to what the good news about Jesus can do.

The stamp says, "You have only one chance for service." Stamps once canceled cannot be used again. That would be an offense. Cards and letters would not go. God has purchased us in Christ for this supreme task of getting the Good News out. We are "canceled" in the sense that we have but one life in which to serve. We cannot expect to do mission work after this life is over. Now is the time to tell it out. Jesus said it like this: "Night comes when no man can work." Getting the Good News out is the "now chance" for people according to Rom. 10:14-17 and Heb. 9:27.

The stamp that is involved in getting the message to its destination has a clear mark of its task. The postmark on the envelope gives the date, time, and year. The year reaches back to the year of our Savior's birth. He came that we might have life. That's the message we share (Col. 1:13-14; Titus 2:11-14). Every day is a day for sharing that news.

We see stamps on letters almost every day. Let each stamp remind us that we are here to share. Some stamps are commemorative stamps, which highlight a big event. We Christians commemorate the great events of God that were involved in the giving of His Son — His birth, death, rising again, and ascension to heaven. Since we know He will come again, we are more urgent about that task.

SEVEN WONDERS
OF THE HOLY SPIRIT

Materials: A candelabrum of seven white candles. Light the candles during the presentation.

Do you know why you so often see a candelabrum with seven candles used in churches? Do you wonder why candles are used at all? The answer is really in the Bible. The Holy Spirit lights up our hearts when He puts faith there. It is the light of God's saving love. The seven candles stand for the seven special gifts the Holy Spirit shares along with faith. Every time they are lighted, we are reminded of those special gifts or wonders of the Holy Spirit. (Gal. 5:22 speaks of the Spirit's gifts. However, this lesson is based on the gifts in Is. 11:2.)

There are seven gifts mentioned in Is. 11:2 that apply to Jesus Christ. According to His human nature He was given the Holy Spirit. This empowered Him to work out the redemption for the world. Whoever believes in Jesus as Savior is born of the Spirit. What is Christ's belongs to believers, as Gal. 4:6 says: "Because you are sons, God has sent the Spirit of His Son into our hearts, crying, 'Abba! Father!' " God the Father gives the same Spirit of His Son to dwell in us. He shares the same wonders.

All human hearts are sinful by nature. They need the Holy Spirit's presence for new life. (Light the first candle.) This stands for the "Spirit of the Lord." When the Holy Spirit takes up His residence in believing hearts, it is so great a wonder that it makes the difference between eternal death and eternal life, between eternal darkness and eternal light, between not being God's sons and being sons. The lighting of the first candle should remind us to thank the Holy Spirit for faith and humbly acknowledge that "I believe that I cannot by my own reason or strength believe in Jesus Christ my Lord or come to Him, but the Holy Spirit has called me by the Gospel, enlightened me with His gifts, sanctified and kept me in the true faith."

The second candle stands for "the spirit of wisdom." By nature all hearts consider Jesus' death on a cross as foolishness (1 Cor. 1:18). The Holy Spirit gives the wisdom to see Jesus' death as personal payment for sin's guilt. That acknowledgement is the wisdom of salvation (2 Tim. 3:15). O Holy Spirit,

> Convince us of our sin,
> Then lead to Jesus' blood,
> And to our wond'ring view reveal
> The mercies of our God.
> (*The Lutheran Hymnal, 225*)

The Pentecost event (Acts 2) shows how mightily the Holy Spirit imparted wisdom. The people of Israel were blinded to the realities of the salvation of Jesus. Then they "wised up" with the Spirit and were saved. (See also Acts 6:1-8)

The third candle stands for "understanding." It is a wonder to know Jesus as Savior, and another wonder to appreciate Him. He is the Pearl of great price. We learn to treasure Him. It is a wonder to know from the Bible that all Christians should tell others of Jesus. But it is still another wonder to have understanding enough to do it because we appreciate what Jesus does for us. It has been said that sometimes Christians have just enough religion to make them miserable. The gift of understanding puts faith into joyful action. It is a wonder to know that the Holy Spirit comes through the means of grace, and another wonder to understand it enough to act: appreciate Baptism, hear and read the Bible, and to remember Holy Communion. (1 Thessalonians 1)

The fourth candle stands for the "spirit of counsel." Jesus called the Holy Spirit a Comforter. It really means a Counselor. When our hearts feel guilty over the wrongs we do, and when we are troubled by life's problems, the Holy Spirit counsels us to look to Jesus. Then guilt, trouble, and boredom give way to victory and service. (Rom. 8:26-39)

The fifth candle is "might." "Not by might (human) nor by power, but by My Spirit, says the Lord of hosts" (Zech. 4:6). You can shout at a ball game by human might, but to shout Christ's praises can be done only in the power of the Holy Spirit. When you feel like a blob, and don't feel like singing Jesus' praises, remember what Jesus did for you. He rescued you with His victory from the devil's rule. That's worth shouting about, isn't it? Serve Jesus with the "might" of Spirit-filled thanksgiving. (Rom. 8:1-17)

The sixth candle stands for "knowledge." It means practical knowledge. It is one thing to know there is a God, and another wonder to know Him as Father, who loves and cares for us and relieves our worries. It is one thing to know that Jesus takes our sins away, another wonder to ask Him to take over the rule of our hearts to fill them with spiritual virtues. It is one thing to know that life is short, but another wonder to act upon that knowledge and get dressed in Jesus' robe of righteousness and then walk in the light of heaven.

The seventh candle stands for "the fear of the Lord." Some people may live as if there were no God, no morals, no Christ, no Judgment Day. Yet these are real! They should realize with dread fear the condemnation of falling into the hands of the living God without faith in Christ. The Holy Spirit makes every believer in Christ a son of God. Believers stand in awe of God. That is the "fear of the Lord" which the Holy Spirit gives along with faith. And so we pray:

> Spirit of Adoption,
> Make us overflow
> With Thy sevenfold blessing
> And in grace to grow.
> (*The Lutheran Hymnal*, 229)

SPIRIT-FILLED CHRISTIANS

Materials: A pair of red-cuffed canvas gloves, used and soiled.

(Display the right-hand glove by holding it in your left hand.) Notice that this glove is empty, limp, and naturally not doing its job. What else do you notice about the glove? It's quite obvious, isn't it? It looks a mess! Let us think of this glove as representing you and me. When we come into this world, we are sinful and unclean. Besides, we lack the Spirit and life of God. We are not fulfilling our purpose either. (Ps. 51:5; John 3:6; Eph. 2:1-3). The apostle Paul reminds Christians at Ephesus that "your old nature belongs to your former manner of life and is corrupt through deceitful lusts" (4:22). As little as this glove can do to get to the hand, so little can we do to come to God. The hand must come to the glove. So now let us think of my hand standing for the Holy Spirit. My hand is alive. It has power. So my hand enters the glove. (Put doubled fist into palm of glove). Receiving Spirit life is a gift of God. This comes by saying yes to Jesus as Savior who forgives my sinful condition. (1 Cor. 12:3; 2 Thess. 2:14)

It is a wonderful truth of the Bible that when a person receives Jesus Christ as Savior, the Holy Spirit comes into the believer's heart and life. Yet it is possible to resist the Holy Spirit's effort to fill our entire life. Look at this glove. You will not deny that my hand is in this glove, will you? Who will come up and shake hands with me? It's not very inviting! If I want to take hold of a handle and go to work, it's next to impossible. A hand that is rolled up into a fist is a dangerous thing. It is more like a horse's hoof that can kick and hurt. When Christianity is rolled up in selfishness, it finds many things to kick about. It's not very serviceable either. Think of the disciples before Pentecost. They had the Holy Spirit for faith. Yet they did not submit to the power of the Holy Spirit. They were self-willed. They argued about human greatness to the very gates of the garden. (Luke 22:24-27)

Jesus went to the garden and the cross for the purpose of redeeming lost, messed-up mankind for God's purposes. The price of this redemption was Jesus' precious blood. We might let this red cuff remind us that we are redeemed at a great price, His blood! This gives the Spirit the right to enter in and reclaim lost lives for God's purposes. So when the disciples took another look at the price of their redemption, they resigned themselves to that amazing love. They prayed more and worshiped more. But more was not enough to fulfill God's purposes, so Pentecost came. (The word means "fiftieth" — the fiftieth day after Easter). Read about this in Acts 2. The important thing about it is that they were all filled with the Spirit. The wind and the fire were but God's audiovisuals to get people's attention. These externals are not experienced by us today, but the presence and fullness of the Spirit can be. So if we take a glance at the disciples after being filled with the Spirit, we see a drastic change for good. God's purposes took priority.

(Put thumb in place.) Let the Spirit fill our worship life. The thumb is the captain of the hand. Fingers bow to the thumb. In worship we present our body and life and everything to God (Rom. 12:1-2). Hearing God's Word, praying, and singing now had new meaning for the disciples. Their hearts were warmed as the "blood" of spiritual life began to circulate by the Spirit's power. Let's remember that Pentecost happened at a church service, not on a golf course or on a picnic.

(Put first finger in glove.) This is the pointer finger. It stands for our first purpose, to point others to Christ. This might be called witness. The disciples spoke freely to others about Jesus Christ. Do we point the way to Christ for others? Jesus said we should. (Acts 1:8)

(Put second finger in place.) This is the tallest finger. It is most noticeable. It is like a leader. The Holy Spirit wants us to lead others in Christ's way by a good example. We might call this sanctification of life. When we aim to live honest and true lives, this shows others the way to Christ. The Holy Spirit sanctifies our hearts. He helps us do good works. (Rom. 15:16; 1 Cor. 6:11; 1 Thess. 4:3)

(Put third finger in place.) This is the ring finger. It reminds us that the Holy Spirit desires to fill our family life, our home life, and every aspect of our daily life. He wants to make our homes a place of true happiness, joy, and service. Children find the home the first church, where the first and most impressive Christian truths are taught by word and example. He wants every family member to live in the joy of Jesus. So kicking and hurting is put aside. True concern for others begins at home with true love between each member. Is your family life filled with the Spirit? (1 Peter 3:1-7; Col. 3:12-25)

(Put fourth finger in place.) The little finger represents the little things we do to make life nice. We send a cheer card to a sick or lonely person. We help a family in need. We greet strangers at church. We pick up someone else's clothes around the house without being asked. The Holy Spirit wants to fill our leisure time, our recreation, and every part of our lives. "So, whether you eat or drink or whatever you do, do all to the glory of God." (1 Cor. 10:31)

Now this hand is ready for real work. (Put on other

glove.) Notice that this glove is not a silk glove. It is a canvas glove made for real hard work. We are made Christians to work for Jesus. (Eph. 2:8-10). But I can also greet others in a friendly handshake (Rom. 12:9-13). (Demonstrate.)

Read Acts 6 about the Spirit-filled deacons. Read about Peter and John in Acts 2 to 5, especially Peter. Think what a change came to his life. Before the Spirit-filling he was afraid of a gatekeeper, now he speaks to crowds and stands up before civil rulers confessing the saving power of Jesus. Read Ezekiel 37; dry bones became alive with the Spirit.

God commands each of us: "Be filled with the Spirit." (Eph. 5:18)

SPIRITUAL HOUSECLEANING

Materials: A house broom, dustpan, and paper sack. If you wish to demonstrate with actual sweeping, use some of the items mentioned in the lesson: glass, cereal, and small clumps of dirt.

Most homes have various items for housecleaning. Vacuum cleaners, dust mops, dust cloths, wet mops, and brooms make up the general supply. Most homes have specified times for housecleaning. So with our hearts, as Christians, we keep up a housecleaning program of repentance. This action comes about when we are faced with God's Law/Gospel Word and speak to Him in prayer at home or at church. In repentance we confess our sins to God and ask for His cleansing (1 John 1:7-9). But there are times in our homes between the times of housecleaning that emergencies come up, don't they? Things get broken or spilled. Dirt gets tracked in. That calls for the broom! So the broom stands for on-the-spot or directed, repentance. This is how it works.

You are helping in the home. Setting the table perhaps. Someone bumps you. You break a glass. There is broken glass all over. You get the broom and sweep it up. So with your Christian life. Things are going fine, and you are enjoying life. Then all of a sudden someone says something that really goes against your grain. You lose your cool! You get angry. You yell and scream. You feel so hateful. Feelings of others are hurt too. That's like breaking a glass. It splatters all over. This calls for the broom of directed repentance. You admit on the spot that your actions were sin in God's sight. You ask forgiveness and accept it, you then find the inner power to go on in the joy of salvation. (1 Peter 3:4)

You are eating your breakfast. You reach and spill some cereal. You get the broom! You are making progress as a Christian. You keep trying to put the best construction on everything you hear about others. You try to say what's good and helpful about others too. Then your tongue slips. A harmful piece of gossip slips out that really hurts your neighbor. That's like spilling the cereal. This calls for directed repentance. Get the broom. Otherwise it just gets tracked around.

In your Christian life you are trying to think about the things that are lovely and pure (Phil. 4:6-8). Then you accept a friend's invitation to see a new movie, with not the highest rating. You got a real kick out of some of the scenes. It was funny at the time. Then you found those "funny" things arising in your mind quite often, and your imagination came up with some very impure thoughts. You then let out these thoughts when talking to others. That's like tracking in dirt. When the "dirt" of the world's ways shows up in the living room of your heart, that's time for broom action.

Another example might be this: You are busy in your housecleaning schedule cleaning the floors and woodwork, and time goes by so fast. You neglect to look to the corners of the ceilings. Cobwebs have accumulated. The broom is real handy to get them down. In your life you are busy with all sorts of Christian activity. Then comes a period of trouble in your family. You find yourself fretting and worrying. You complain and act rather moody. Then you realize that "cobwebs" have been accumulating. This calls for the broom.

If we let the glass, cereal, dirt and cobwebs accumulate,

what a horrible mess our homes would be in! The accumulation would be too much for the mops and vacuum cleaner. When a home gets too messed up, it deserves a condemned sign. And if nothing happens to change it, you know what happens. A bulldozer comes and destroys it. The Bible says that unrepented sin leads to condemnation. (John 3:17-21)

So before we will use the broom of directed repentance, we have to be sold on cleanliness. True spiritual housecleaning comes by the power of the Holy Spirit. It is practiced when we realize that as Christians we have a very honored Guest in our hearts. Our motto is, "A clean heart for a holy Guest, Jesus." When we become Christians and know the cleansing of Jesus Christ by faith (sin's guilt is washed away) then we want Christ to cleanse our hearts more and more of all sin.

The apostle John said: "Everyone who thus hopes in Him purifies himself as He is pure" (1 John 3:3). John also said: "No one born of God commits sin" (1 John 3:9). He means that Christians do not purposely practice sin. Christians aim to practice cleanliness of heart and life. This is done by daily repentance, which turns to God and asks for forgiveness of all sins, even those which we do not see.

Heb. 12:1 (KJV) speaks of "besetting" sins. If we keep such sins cleaned from our lives by directed, on-the-spot repentance, our lives will be a lot cleaner for Jesus' glory, happier for ourselves, and nicer for other people. (Phil. 4:6-8; Ps. 119:9)

Brooms are made and must be purchased. Jesus gives us "brooms" of repentance when He gives us His Holy Spirit (Luke 24:46-47; Acts 5:30-31). Zechariah and Elizabeth (Luke 1:6), Simeon (Luke 2:25), Anna (Luke 2:36-38) are some of the "broom people" of the Bible. Rom. 12:

1-2 says we can all be that kind of people. Keep the broom handy. Every time you see or use the broom, think about the spiritual housecleaning of your heart.

STRENGTH IN SUFFERING

Materials: A number of toothpicks and a nail the length of the toothpicks. One toothpick should be straight to represent Job. Three should be bent and twisted to represent Job's friends. One should be partly bent for Elihu. Others, left straight, will be used for other Christians at the opening and closing of the lesson.

(Give a child a straight toothpick.) This toothpick is to represent a person. As you hold it in your hand, let your other hand become the power of adversity which befalls people in this life. Your hand can bend, twist, and even break this toothpick. (Demonstrate it.) So adversity, which brings suffering, can do the same. One way to strengthen this toothpick would be to add several more. Here is a bunch. (Add five or six.) The outcome is still the same. (Show how the whole bunch can be twisted, bent, and even broken.)

Now I want you to hold this toothpick. It's straight. It stands for a person who lived long ago. He was blameless and upright, one who feared God and turned away from evil (Job 1:1). His name was Job. He was a very rich man. He had a lovely wife, ten children; a lot of livestock (1:2-3). One day the sun came up and all was bright as usual. Then reports came to him that his livestock was stolen and destroyed. Then that his children were destroyed in the manor house by a freak storm. But Job stood tall. He said: "The Lord gave, and the Lord has taken away; blessed be the name of the Lord" (1:21). Shortly after that sickness struck

135

his body. He was full of pain. He looked a mess. Ugly boils all over! His wife left him. He was put out on the city dump. She said: "Curse God and die" (2:9). In all that pain he wondered why he was born anyway. He said: "Let the day perish wherein I was born" (3:3). And he thought it best to die (6:8-9). (Compare 10:18; 14:1-2.) He began to bend under the power of suffering. (Bend the toothpick a little.) So it seems that he needed some help to hold up in the suffering.

Some of Job's friends from far away heard about his troubles. They were Eliphaz, Bildad, and Zophar. They came to comfort Job. These three toothpicks represent the three friends. (Hold the three twisted toothpicks next to the Job toothpick.) Maybe you are wondering why they are so twisted and bent like that. That is to represent their thinking and what they said about suffering. It was far from straight. They broke all rules in visiting the sick too. They stared at the patient, stayed too long, and pointed accusing fingers. Their long visit is recorded in Job 4 to 31, which also has Job's conversation. But they did most of the talking. They reasoned like this: "All suffering is punishment for sin. It is sent by God. If your grief is great and you are suffering greatly, then there is proof positive you are a great sinner." So they urged Job to confess. Job kept saying that he was living in repentance with his heart open to God and trusting His loving forgiveness. They pointed fingers, "You are doing away with the fear of God . . . your iniquity teaches your mouth, and you choose the tongue of the crafty" (15:4-5). Then they accused him of being punished for sins in proportion to a man in his position of riches — not curing all the social ills (22:7). So their "theology of suffering" did more harm than good. He was led to complain (19:14) and to question the ways of God. (10:18)

Another person overheard the miserable advice of the

136

three friends. His name was Elihu. He added insult to injury. He broke the rules of visiting too. He stayed too long. (His speech is in chapters 32 to 37.) His idea was that God sends suffering and sorrow to discourage people from sinning (34:31-32 is a good sample). (Add Elihu toothpick.) So here we have the miserable comforters trying to help Job. It's a real twisted mess, isn't it? What could bring strength?

Now, I want to show you something that will add strength to this toothpick. It's a nail. (Place it next to the Job toothpick and try to break the toothpick.) The powers and pressures of suffering cannot break a person who has his strength in God. We will let this nail stand for God. During the suffering Job cursed his birthday, but he did not curse God. He questioned, but he did not lose faith in God. He began to bend, but was not broken. He rather said some great things about God: "Though He slay me, yet will I trust in Him" (13:15 KJV). He also saw beyond the grave to eternal victory (19:26-27). He had great faith in God's love and purposes. Yet Job should not have questioned the ways of God. So God spoke to Job from the whirlwind (chapters 38 to 41). God reminded Job that he didn't even understand things in nature around him, like rain clouds, the mystery of the snowflakes, the majesty of the eagle, the strength of the horse, hippopotamus, and crocodile. Job realized anew that it is impossible to understand the ways of God. Rather that His dealings with His believers is a matter of faith. After his suffering he saw God's love more clearly. He said: "Now my eye sees Thee . . . and I repent in dust and ashes." (42:5-6)

What good does God accomplish in letting Satan perplex us with grief and suffering? One thing is sure. It's not punishment for sin. God in love let all punishment fall on His Son. He was nailed to the cross and paid the penalty for sin in full (Is. 53:4-5). So suffering and sorrow are "mercy reminders" of God's love and His eternal purpose (Rom. 8:28). With faith we accept God's ways of love (Is. 55:8-9). Elihu came quite close to this truth (37:23). But he was more excited about God's power than His love. We are to remember that God loved us so much as to send His Son to save us for heaven. And He will also keep us mindful of how much we need that love day by day. Knowing that God's ways are always ways of love, let us go to the sick and suffering with that assurance.

God blessed Job with health, a new family, and many possessions, plus a long life. The trial perhaps was necessary to keep Job from falling in love with riches. God only knows the real reason. For us it is enough that we trust Him at all times.

> Judge not the Lord by feeble sense,
> But trust Him for His grace,
> Behind a frowning providence
> He hides a smiling face.
> *(The Lutheran Hymnal,* 514)

There are other examples of strength in suffering in the Bible. Joseph suffered (Genesis 37 and 39). His faith was purified by it (Gen. 50:20-21). The apostle Paul suffered and found God's grace sufficient (2 Cor. 12:7-10). Peter suffered with his fellow Christians, but triumphed by trust. (1 Peter 1:5-9)

THE TEN COMMANDMENTS

Materials: A strip of white paper long enough to accordion-fold and cut out ten hearts that will be hinged
together. (Adding machine paper is excellent; however,
if you desire larger hearts, use wider and longer paper.)
Write the positive summary words of the commandments on the hearts. (God, God's Name, God's Word;
Authority, Life, Purity, Honesty, Truth, Contentment,
Helpfulness.) Write in blue for loyalty. The words should
be on the outside when the hearts are joined in a circle.
You will need a wooden or cardboard cross and a thumb
tack and a white heart the same size as the commandment hearts.

(Display the circle of hearts.) The Bible says that
"love is the fulfilling of the Law" (Rom. 13:10). This means
that by loving God and others perfectly you would be fulfilling God's holy will. God has revealed His will to us in
ten precepts or commandments. So we have ten hearts
joined together. This forms a circle to remind us that His
commands are His eternal will. Blue lettering indicates that
God desires our perfect loyalty. Let us review the summary
concepts of the Law. (Pupils may read the summary
words. Add explanations where necessary.) Now I shall
tell you a true story from the Bible. I want you to write
down the commandment that was broken by using the
summary word or number as I tell you the story.

A man by the name of Naboth lived in a town called
Jezreel. He was a godly man. He owned some land that

bordered on the palace property of the king. The king's name was Ahab. His wife's name was Jezebel. Naboth raised vegetables on his land. The civil law given by God said that land of the people of Israel should be kept in the family, not sold. King Ahab viewed the fine vegetables Naboth raised. He set his heart on having the land. He owned much land and was very rich. But he wanted Naboth's vineyard. He offered to buy it for a fair price or trade a good vineyard for it. Naboth could not sell; the king went home vexed and wouldn't eat. He complained to Jezebel. She assured him that everything would be just fine.

She wrote letters in Ahab's name and sealed them with his seal. The letters were to the city officials. They were told to bring Naboth to trial. They were instructed to hire professional liars to say that Naboth had cursed God and the king. He should therefore be killed. This was done. Jezebel reported to Ahab that he should take possession of the vineyard because Naboth was dead. Ahab took the garden for himself. (1 Kings 21:1-16)

Which ones were broken? (As commandments are indicated as broken, tear off the heart near the hinge.) Ahab coveted the garden and did not help his neighbor keep what was his (9 and 10). Jezebel deceived, lied, and said untruths about Naboth (2 and 8). Jezebel went against God's word about the land and against the king's authority. Which commandments were involved here? (3 and 4). Jezebel had Naboth murdered (5). Behind all that was the fact that King Ahab and Queen Jezebel did not love God. They broke the First Commandment! They stole the property (7). There's one commandment left, the sixth. But just how pure is a person who would do all that? The purity commandment includes more than keeping sex pure. It has to do with moral purity, don't you think? So they broke six too. All the commandments were broken by two people in this account.

The Bible teaches that if you break but one commandment, you become guilty of all (James 2:10). One link broken spoils a chain. One commandment broken spoils the circle of love. But usually one sin involves others. Breaking one commandment involves breaking others. If a person cheats or steals, he usually lies to cover it up. When a person desires falsehood rather than truth, he really does not love and trust God above all things. Think about some situations in your life.

God wants to convince us that we all are commandment-breakers by nature. He wants us to own up to our guilt before Him (1 John 1:8-10). The Law becomes a mirror that shows us our sinfulness and our need for God's forgiveness. (Rom. 3:20; Ps. 14:3; Is. 64:6)

God has provided the one way to find release from the guilt of law-breaking. "God has forgiven us all our trespasses, having canceled the bond which stood against us with its legal demands; this He set aside, nailing it to the cross" (Col. 2:13-14). (Tack the broken "hearts" to the cross.) Isn't it most gracious of God to give us such a complete forgiveness? As we believe in Jesus Christ, we are given new hearts. (Hold the white heart over the broken, "heart-commandments.") God sees each of us as if we never had broken His laws. (1 Peter 2:24, 3:18; Gal. 3:10-14, 21-22; 1 Tim. 2:5-6)

Because we have new hearts, we desire to show our love to God in Christ. Love is our motive. This means that our new heart desires the will of God (Jer. 31:33-34). So the white of our new heart reminds us that we aim to identify with God's commandments, which make known His holy will. As Christians we uphold God's law. The Law that serves as a mirror to show us our sins and our need for pardon is also a rule for Christian living.

You can read about how owning up to guilt and having it forgiven leads to desiring God's ways (Psalm 32; Eph. 2:8-9). Psalm 119 is a prayer about this. You will find the Ten Commandments in Ex. 20:1-17. Let us strive to live them better and better.

THE TIE THAT BINDS

Materials: Two paper strips 3' long and 2" wide (use adding machine paper, if handy). At one place in each strip paste a red heart about 2" high. You will need a standing cross. Link the two strips together as you give one end of each a half turn. Place the links at the base of the cross with the upright beam between the links as shown in illustration. You will also need a pair of scissors.

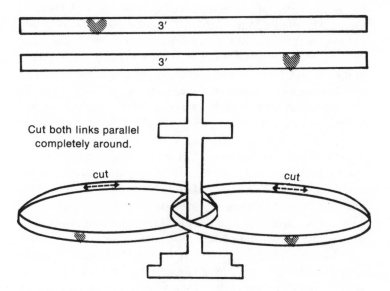

Cut both links parallel completely around.

cut   cut

Pull each circle carefully to tighten the tie around the cross after cutting.

These two links joined together at the cross remind us of Christian love. The hearts on the links stand for love (red because it has its source in the Calvary love of Christ). Christian love is referred to as "the tie that binds." The Bible speaks of Christian love as an imitation of God's love for us in Christ. God loved the world of sinful people so much that He gave His own Son for their salvation. When we experience God's love in our hearts by faith, we begin to love in the "quality" of His love. This love is devoted to others in spite of their unworthiness. That love is kind and forgiving. It seeks the highest good for others. That love is described in 1 Corinthians 13, the love chapter of the Bible. Verses 4 to 8 define that love in action. Someone has said that you should read that section by first substituting the name of Jesus for love because He is the love of God personified (John 10:14, 17; Rom. 5:6-8). Then as you believe in Jesus as your Savior, put your name in the place of love, for love flows from faith. See what a great calling you have in Christ! When you aim to practice this love, you will have genuine concern for others. (Rom. 12:9; 13:8-10)

Christian love is truly enduring. It can endure insults, hardships, and attacks of evil. We will let the scissors stand for the threats of evil that seek to cut the tie that binds. Scissors are real "enemies" of paper, aren't they? When the "scissors of evil" cut the tie of Christian love, the unusual happens. (Cut each link in half parallel, or around the middle.) Notice that the ties are now double-tied around the cross. The threats of evil only make the tie that binds even tighter. Think of some Bible examples.

The disciples of Jesus were told in the Upper Room to love one another in the love of Christ (John 13:34-35). This would give them strength to face an evil, threatening world. This would be a badge of the genuineness of the Gospel. They experienced the togetherness of Christian love in worship (Acts 1:12-14). Compare some thoughts in John's epistles (1 John 4:11-12, 20-21). Think about their lives in testimony of the Gospel. The pagan world had to admit, "Behold, how they love one another!" Early Christians enjoyed that love (Acts 2:42-47; 8:1-4). When persecuted, they still stayed tied to their Lord and Master and to each other in His service.

Jonathan and David had the tie that binds. "The soul of Jonathan was knit to the soul of David, and Jonathan loved him as his own soul" (1 Sam. 18). Saul tried to cut the bond of love by attempting to kill David, but it only tied them closer together. (See 1 Sam. 19)

John and Mary were tied in Christian love. When Jesus was dying on the cross to redeem the world, He thought of His mother Mary. He would not tell her to go to the home of His half-brother or -sisters (Matt. 13:55-56; Mark 6:4). Since they did not believe in Him as Savior, there was no Christian love there. Believing Mary should enjoy a home where Christian love abounds, so He commended her to John, the apostle of love (John 20:25-27). Their bond of friendship in Christ was greater than family ties.

The tie that binds is the power for happy marriages. (Eph. 5:21-33)

The "scissors of evil" cannot harm Christian love. Life goes better with love.

THREE CROSSES OF CALVARY

Materials: A piece of paper in the proportion of 5½" by 8½" (as large as you desire). The front side dark gray. The back side divided into equal portions of thirds. The center third red, the outside thirds, one gray and one white. After you display the gray side in the introduction you will accordion-fold into thirds and then fold according to directions. (Always show gray side to the audience as you fold.)

Paper accordion-folded.

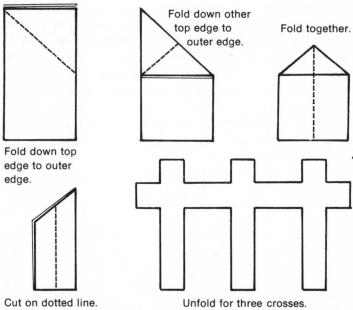

Fold down top edge to outer edge.

Fold down other top edge to outer edge.

Fold together.

Cut on dotted line.

Unfold for three crosses.

Here is a piece of gray paper. Let us associate this color with the greatest human problem. ~~Can you tell what it is?~~ Yes, it is the problem of death. Isaiah speaks of it as thick darkness (Is. 60:2). Jesus called it outer darkness (Matt. 25:30). Death is serious business because it comes in three dimensions: spiritual, lack of divine life; physical, separation of soul and body; and eternal, total separation from God—unless something happens to change it.

Something did happen. Praise God! God sent His Son to die the sinners' death penalty. We can read about this in Luke 23:32-45. (Fold paper into thirds and fold for the crosses and cut.) (Display as one cross.) God's Son died the cross-death. It was most painful, and of course most shameful. To die on a cross was considered a curse because it was the form of capital punishment in those days. (Unfold other crosses, displaying the gray side.) These two crosses stand for the two criminals who were put to death with Jesus that first Good Friday. Jesus and the two criminals died a physical death that day. The whole scene of Calvary was a curtain of gloom, black and horrible!

But let us take a closer look. How did it look from the other side? (Turn scene around.) What do you notice about the center cross? It is red. "In Him we have redemption through His blood, the forgiveness of our trespasses, according to the riches of His grace" (Eph. 1:7). He took the eternal death penalty of the world's sins to Himself (1 Peter 2:22, 24; Heb. 9:26-30). The center cross stands for self-sacrifice. He died FOR sin.

One of the outer crosses is white. Do you know what that means? One of the criminals owned up to his crimes before God. He was sorry for them. He heard Jesus ask the Father to forgive people. He included himself in that prayer. Furthermore, he saw how patiently Jesus suffered. He recognized it as the suffering of God. He asked Jesus as his God and King: "Remember me when you come into your kingly power." Jesus said: "Truly, today you will be with Me in Paradise." He made an act of self-surrender. He died TO sin. His soul was saved. He was changed from spiritual death to spiritual life. He was spared the second death, which is eternal (Rev. 20:6; John 5:24-25). Physical death became the gateway to glory.

The other cross is gray. The other criminal experienced three deaths. He died IN sin and selfishness. He even mocked the Savior (Luke 23:39). He lived only for himself. He committed crimes against others. He had no room for the love of God or the pardon of the Savior. He was lost by his own fault. (John 3:36)

Let us always remember that the sinless Son of God died that we sinful people might have spiritual life again by faith. This spares us from eternal death. Then physical death (unless Jesus comes in glory first) is the door to heaven. Physical death has lost its power to hurt (1 Cor. 15:55-56). Jesus rose from physical death, so our bodies too shall rise. The death of God's Son was so terrible as He tasted death for everyone that God let darkness cover the whole land for three hours as if He pulled down the shades. Let us never forget what Jesus saves us from. Let us thank and praise Him always for giving us spiritual life, which means eternal life. (John 3:36)

(Cut off the gray cross.) Eternal death is separation from the Savior. Eternal life is being with Him forever.

THREE PILLARS
OF THE REFORMATION

Materials: A miniature gold cross and a child.

Dear child, I love you and therefore I want to give you a gift. The gift is in my hand. (Keep the cross out of sight in the clenched hand.) This gift is something you will cherish. It stands for the greatest blessing anyone can receive. Do you want this gift? If you do you will have to reach out your hand to receive it. But before you reach out your hand you must believe that I have such a gift. In other words, you must accept my word as good and true. Besides that, you don't take gifts from strangers, do you? I'm no stranger to you, am I? I am your friend and as a Christian teacher I speak the truth. So reach out your hand and receive it. The gold cross is yours.

Now let's review this transaction. Did you do anything for me to earn my love and win my favor? No. It could be that you even disappointed me in class. And you deserved something other than a gift. The fact that you have this gift is an act of grace on my part. Giving something precious to someone who doesn't deserve it, that's the meaning of the word grace. God gives forgiving love to undeserving sinners. He does this because He placed the punishment for sin on His dear Son. It says in Rom. 3:23-25: "Since all have sinned and fall short of the glory of God, they are justified by His grace as a gift, through the redemption which is in Christ Jesus, whom God put forward as an expiation by His blood, to be received by faith." It says in

Eph. 2:8-9: "For by grace you have been saved . . . this is not your own doing, it is the gift of God — not because of works."

The fact that you reached out your hand meant that you believed what I said about my offer to you. That was faith on your part. You did not have that faith until I told you about that precious gift which symbolized your greatest need and blessing. The Bible tells us that it is only by faith in Jesus Christ that we are saved. The Eph. 2:8 section says: "For by grace you have been saved through faith." The Rom. 3:23-25 section says that we "are justified by His grace as a gift . . . to be received by faith." The apostle Paul says in Rom. 1:16-17: "I am not ashamed of the Gospel: it is the power of God for salvation to every one who has faith . . . . For in it the righteousness of God is revealed through faith for faith; as it is written, 'He who through faith is righteous shall live.' " Faith is taking God at His word. It is a divinely worked assurance in our hearts that says, "Yes, Jesus, You are my Savior. Your righteousness covers me. I accept it."

Think about the transaction again. It involved my word, didn't it? Without my telling you, you would not know that I had a gift for you. It took my words to reveal my offer. So with God to us. God speaks to us in His Word, the Bible. It proclaims His offer of love. It is all about His grace in the cross of Jesus Christ, in His life, death, and resurrection. It is foretold in the Old Testament in the Law and the Prophets. It is fulfilled in the New Testament in the gospels and the epistles. God says that His word is sufficient to bring us to faith: "Now Jesus did many other signs in the presence of the disciples, which are not written in this book; but these are written that you may believe that Jesus is the Christ, the Son of God, and that believing you may have life in His name." (John 20:30-31) "The Law and the

Prophets bear witness to it" (Rom. 3:21). (Compare 2 Tim. 3:14-17; Rev. 22:18-19.) God's written Word, the Bible — the 66 books — is enough to reveal God's grace. Another term for the Bible is Holy Scripture.

So we see how the three words grace, faith, and Scripture work together to bring about our salvation. These three words are often called "The Three Pillars of the Reformation." Usually they are lined up like this: Scripture, grace, faith. For emphasis the word "alone" is added: Scripture alone, grace alone, faith alone. These three pillars alone can hold up the structure of the eternal salvation of our souls. When we abide by these words, then a genuine reformation goes on where it really counts — in our souls.

Martin Luther discovered by reading the Bible carefully and letting God speak to him that His Word alone was sufficient to bring a person to faith. He found that the central truth of God's Word was God's grace in Christ. He found that faith was not a meritorious work on the part of man, but the Spirit-worked assurance in the hearts of believers. This faith gives people new birth and new life (Titus 3:4-7). Luther found himself a born-again child of God. In his writings he remarked: "You must boldly take your stand on His words. This is my rock and anchor. The word must stand, for God cannot lie. . . . There is no salvation, except by simply believing in Christ, believing that He alone has rendered satisfaction for our sin, has gained grace and saved us solely through His merit."

Grace spelled as an acrostic says, "God's riches at Christ's expense." That's what the cross is all about. So, dear child, cherish the cross as the symbol of God's gift of grace. Cherish Christ as your personal Savior in your heart.

By grace! This ground of faith is certain;
So long as God is true, it stands.

What saints have penned by inspiration,
What in His Word our God commands,
What our whole faith must rest upon,
Is grace alone, grace in His Son.
                    (*The Lutheran Hymnal*, 373)

Some Bible accounts which show the three pillars at work in lives of people are: Num. 2:4-9 compared with John 3:14-17; Is. 6:1-8; Hab. 2:1-4; John 4:46-54; Acts 8:26-40; and Acts 16:25-34.

TWO LIFE-STYLES

Materials: Two gray capital *I* letters 14″ high made from gray construction paper. The stems should be an inch wide, and the top and bottom bars should be 4″ wide and an inch high. Make the back of one *I* red by pasting red construction paper to it. This *I* will represent the publican-tax collector. During the presentation this *I* will become a cross when you bend the top bar down 2½″ from the top and the bottom bar up 5″ from the bottom. The cross will be red. The other *I* will represent the Pharisee.

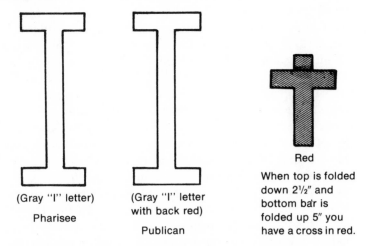

(Gray "I" letter)
Pharisee

(Gray "I" letter with back red)
Publican

Red

When top is folded down 2½″ and bottom bar is folded up 5″ you have a cross in red.

(Display both *I*'s with gray side to audience.) These letters will stand for people. They remind us what is wrong with every person on earth. What is it? "That's easy,"

153

you say, "because the gray gives it away — it's sin." These letters go a bit deeper into the problem of sin and point to the very root of sin. That is pride. As these "I" letters stand up, so sinners boast of their uprightness. Think of the Pharisee in the parable Jesus told (Luke 18:11-12). "The Pharisee stood and prayed thus with himself, 'God, I thank thee that I am not like other men, extortioners, unjust, adulterers, or even like this tax collector. I fast twice a week, I give tithes of all that I get.'" Notice how often he said "I." Think of Saul, the persecutor of the early church (Acts 9:1; Phil. 3:4b-6). He acted like a religious "big shot." The letter *I* goes way back to the fall into sin by Adam and Eve. They followed the advice of Satan when he suggested that to disobey God would make them wise as God. This was pride. Satan himself fell because he desired to be like the Most High (Is. 14:12-15). God has a word for the proud: "The Lord of hosts has a day against all that is proud and lofty, against all that is lifted up" (Is. 2:12). That day is the day of wrath (John 3:36b). (Read about Absalom's pride, 2 Sam. 14:25 — 15:6 and chapter 18.)

The opposite of pride is humility. That attitude is possible when a sinner compares himself to the holiness of God. Once a sinful tax collector went to the temple. Everything about the place spoke of reverence for God and holiness. He thought of himself as compared to God. He acted. Jesus said: "The tax collector, standing far off, would not even lift up his eyes to heaven, but beat his breast, saying, 'God be merciful to me a sinner!'" (Luke 18:13). He was sorry for his sins. He bent over in humility. (Bend the top bar of the tax collector *I* down and the bottom bar up.) His cry for God's mercy was most meaningful. God can have mercy only through Christ. What the tax collector really said was, "God, may my debt for sins be paid." He prayed in full view of the temple sacrifices — the shedding of the lamb's blood which pictured the blood of the Son of God that would be shed for the sins of the world. The Son of God, as the great Lamb of God, paid the debt of all sins for every sinner. The persecutor Saul humbled himself too (Acts 9:2-22; Phil. 3:7-11; Gal. 2:20). So Jesus said: "I tell you, this man went down to his house justified [right with God] rather than the other; for everyone who exalts himself will be humbled, but he who humbles himself will be exalted." (Luke 18:14; Prov. 29:23)

There is a Pharisee in the hearts of all of us. The tax collector needed both the Law and Gospel — the Law to know his spiritual need and the Gospel to know God's mercy. The Pharisee in us wants us to pray, "God, I thank You that I am not like that nasty Pharisee." But when we hear God's Word, both the Law and the Gospel, then we can pray:

> When I survey the wondrous cross
> On which the Prince of Glory died,
> My richest gain I count but loss
> And pour contempt on all my pride.
> (*The Lutheran Hymnal,* 175)

There are really two types of people in the world: Sinners who think they are saints, and saints who know they are sinners. The latter know they need Christ, who paid their debt of sin. Which type are you? You can either look into God's holy law and then admit you are a sinner, or you can look to your weak neighbor and then thank God you aren't as bad as he is. The tax collector's prayer arose from the former, and the Pharisee's prayer from the latter. How will you pray? Which life-style is yours?

Adapted from *Talking Object Lessons*
Zondervan Publishing House
Used by permission

THE WISE STILL WORSHIP CHRIST

Materials: A white or yellow five-pointed star made from 8½" by 11" paper. Fold down the two top points. Fold side points to center. Fold together. Cut one half inch on long side. Unfold. You have a cross. Fold down the top of the cross and you have *T* for truth. Fold *T* together, and you have an *L* for life.

Fold two top points down.

Fold side points to center, downward and inward.

Fold together.

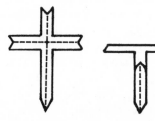

Cut along dotted line. Unfold.

The cross is the Way.

T for Truth Fold top down.

L for Life Fold together.

(Display star.) The five-pointed star which adorns tops of Christmas trees and is seen in so many places at Christmastime is called the Bethlehem Star. It symbolizes the special star that God sent to lead the Wise Men to Jesus. We read: "Now when Jesus was born in Bethlehem of Judea in the days of Herod the king, behold, Wise Men from the East came to Jerusalem, saying, 'Where is He who has been born king of the Jews? For we have seen His star in the East and have come to worship Him.'" (Matt. 2:1-2)

Since these men came from the East, they probably had heard about the coming of the Savior from God's people who had been there in captivity centuries before. Like the ancient people of those countries, these men were interested in the stars. Stars were thought of as symbols of kingship and government. Thus with the appearance of a special star, they were led to believe that a king had been born.

There is no reason to think that the Bethlehem Star was a natural phenomenon. That star was very unusual and special. It guided them westward for many days during the long journey. Then it stopped and waited for them in Jerusalem. It made a turn to lead them to Bethlehem. It stopped over the very house where the child Jesus was. So it was God's "miracle star" that led the Wise Men.

What did they find by following the leading of the star? I shall fold the star in this fashion and cut it. There it is! A cross! They found Him who is the way of salvation. They accepted Him as their Savior-King. Their very gifts: gold, frankincense, and myrrh, show that they knew Him to be their King, God, and Sacrifice. (Gold symbolized worship of Him as King. Frankincense, a fragrant gum used in Old Testament temple sacrifices, symbolized Him as the God who hears prayer. Myrrh, used for embalming, symbolized His sacrificial death. (Eph. 5:1-2; John 20:39-40.)

These men are called "Wise Men." They were wise in the sense that they did not let their earthly position (Is. 60:3-6) mislead them. They were wise in that they followed the star. But the wisdom that really made them wise was given them by the Spirit. "The fear of the Lord is the beginning of wisdom" (Ps. 111:10). Also: "From a child thou hast known the holy Scriptures, which are able to make thee wise unto salvation through faith which is in Christ Jesus" (2 Tim. 3:15 KJV). Jesus is the way to God. Faith in Christ makes Him the object of our worship; the object of our prayers to God, and the object of our dedication.

Many people are wise in their own conceits. The apostle Paul mentioned this. "For the word of the cross is folly to those who are perishing, but to us who are being saved it is the power of God" (1 Cor. 1:18). He explains that Jesus Christ is the source of our life: "Whom God made our wisdom, our righteousness and sanctification and redemption" (1 Cor. 1:30). (Review entire section 1 Cor. 1:18 – 2:16.) The message that saves is about Christ crucified, the hidden wisdom of God revealed by His Spirit, interpreting spiritual truths to those who possess the Spirit. (Show *T* for truth.) There is no other way to know God than through the sacrifice of Jesus on the cross. God is known in His forgiving love by the cross (John 18:37-38). As the Way and the Truth Jesus is our Life. (Show *L* for life.) John 3:16 and 36 express this clearly. Jesus summed this up in John 14:6. The Wise Men found all that wisdom in Jesus.

The Wise Men departed to their own country another way. They had been warned in a dream about Herod's evil plan. And they went the way of a joyful faith. In Acts 9:2 and 19:9 the "Way" means Jesus Christ and His salvation.

There is an old saying about hitching your wagon to a star. Spiritually, we must make sure it is the right Star. Christ is our Star (Num. 24:17). But we must keep the axles of our "wagon" greased for the time when things begin to move. We must move when led, like the Wise Men. They went and found. Led by a star means following the leading of God's Word and providence in concerted action. The wise still worship Christ. Apart from Him there is only death.

> As with gladness men of old
> Did the guiding star behold;
> As with joy they hailed its light,
> Leading onward, beaming bright,
> So, most gracious Lord, may we
> Evermore be led by Thee!
> (*The Lutheran Hymnal,* 127)

Bibliography

De Golia, J. E. *Object Lessons . . . Using Common Things.* Wheaton: Scripture Press, 1954

McLean, W. T. *Illustrated Gospel Object Lessons.* Grand Rapids: Zondervan Publishing House, 1945

Ryrie, Charles C. *Easy-to-Get Object Lessons.* Grand Rapids: Zondervan Publishing House, 1949

Troke, James A. *Object Teaching Made Easy.* Butler: The Higley Press, 1942

Whitwell, Nevada M. *At Home and Abroad: Youth Worship Programs.* Cincinnati: Standard Publishing Company, 1952

Wilder, Elmer L. *Favorite Object Lessons No. 2.* Portland: Christianews Press, 1959

— — —. *See It! Object Lessons.* Grand Rapids: Zondervan Publishing House, 1945

— — —. *Talking Object Lessons.* Grand Rapids: Zondervan Publishing House, 1942